Val Cauthe

The School Mathematics Project

GCSE
Mathematics
Revision

Intermediate Tier

CAMBRIDGE
UNIVERSITY PRESS

PUBLISHED BY THE PRESS SYNDICATE OF THE UNIVERSITY OF CAMBRIDGE
The Pitt Building, Trumpington Street, Cambridge CB2 1RP, United Kingdom

CAMBRIDGE UNIVERSITY PRESS
The Edinburgh Building, Cambridge CB2 2RU, United Kingdom
40 West 20th Street, New York, NY 10011–4211, USA
10 Stamford Road, Oakleigh, Melbourne 3166, Australia

© Cambridge University Press 1997

First published 1997

Printed in the United Kingdom at the University Press, Cambridge

A catalogue record for this book is available from the British Library

ISBN 0 521 57908 2

This book has been written and compiled by

Eric Gower
Bob Hartman
Spencer Instone
Elizabeth Jackson
Paul Scruton

The authors' warm thanks go to the teachers who tested the draft materials in their schools and to Howard Baxter and William Wynne Willson who gave advice from an examiner's standpoint.

Certain questions in this book are reproduced by kind permission of the following:

The Midland Examining Group
The Northern Ireland Council for the Curriculum Examinations and Assessment
The Southern Examining Group
The University of London Examinations and Assessment Council
The Welsh Joint Education Committee

These questions are acknowledged individually in the text. None of the above groups bears any responsibility for the accuracy or method of working in example answers to these questions.

Contents

Formula sheet

Area of triangle = $\frac{1}{2}$ × base x height

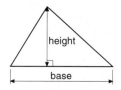

Circumference of circle = $\pi \times$ diameter
$\qquad\qquad\qquad\qquad = 2 \times \pi \times$ radius
Area of circle = $\pi \times$ (radius)^2

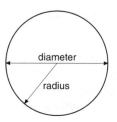

Area of parallelogram = base × height

Area of trapezium = $\frac{1}{2}(a + b)h$

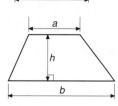

Volume of cuboid = length × width × height

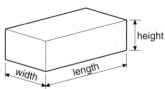

Volume of cylinder = $\pi r^2 h$

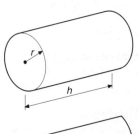

Volume of prism = (area of cross-section) × length

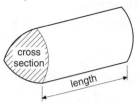

Pythagoras' Theorem
$$a^2 + b^2 = c^2$$

Trigonometry

$$\sin\theta = \frac{\text{opp}}{\text{hyp}}$$

$$\cos\theta = \frac{\text{adj}}{\text{hyp}}$$

$$\tan\theta = \frac{\text{opp}}{\text{adj}}$$

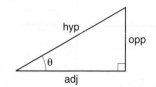

How to use this book

This book covers the content of all the GCSE mathematics syllabuses at
intermediate level. There is a brief explanation of each topic followed by
questions (including many from past GCSE examinations) for you to
work through. You will find answers and hints to all the questions
at the back of the book.

How you use this book depends on how much you need to revise.
It is divided into sections – Number, Algebra, Shape, space and measures
and Handling data. You could start at the beginning of a section and
work through it steadily or you could pick out the things that you are
unsure about (with the help of the contents pages) and concentrate on them.
If you need further help, references to SMP 11–16 books, at the end
of each set of Answers and hints, tell you where to find it.

Some questions need worksheets. Ask your teacher for these.

NUMBER
Properties of numbers

The **factors** of a whole number are those numbers which divide exactly into it. (The factors of 20 are 1, 2, 4, 5, 10 and 20.)

The numbers 3, 6, 9, 12 and 15 are **multiples** of 3; 3 is a factor of each of them.

A number which has only two factors, itself and one, is called a **prime number**. (2, 3, 5 and 7 are all prime numbers, but 1 is not.)

If you multiply some prime numbers together, they are the **prime factors** of the number you get.

$$2 \times 3 \times 3 \times 5 = 90$$

The prime factors of 90

Any number can be split into the product of prime factors. For example:

$$156 = 2 \times 78$$
$$= 2 \times 2 \times 39$$
$$= 2 \times 2 \times 3 \times 13 = 2^2 \times 3 \times 13$$

36 is called the **square** of 6. We write $6 \times 6 = 6^2 = 36$.   36 is a **square number**.

64 is called the **cube** of 4. We write $4 \times 4 \times 4 = 4^3 = 64$.   64 is a **cube number**.

We say that:

6 is the **square root** of 36 and write $\sqrt{36} = 6$.

4 is the **cube root** of 64 and write $\sqrt[3]{64} = 4$.

To find the **reciprocal** of a number you divide 1 by the number.

For example: the reciprocal of 6 is $\frac{1}{6}$

the reciprocal of $\frac{1}{6} = 1 \div \frac{1}{6} = 1 \times \frac{6}{1} = 6$

the reciprocal of $\frac{2}{5} = 1 \div \frac{2}{5} = 1 \times \frac{5}{2} = \frac{5}{2}$

Make sure you can find squares, cubes, square roots and cube roots on your calculator, and can use the reciprocal key – usually $\boxed{1/x}$ *or* $\boxed{x^{-1}}$.

Dividing by a fraction
► **page 8**

1 Look at this list of numbers.

   2   3   16   18   19   25   29   512

   From the list write down

   (a) a multiple of 6   (b) a square number   (c) the cube root of 8

2 (a) Write down all the factors of 24.

   (b) Write down all the prime numbers between 30 and 50.

   (c) Write down all the cube numbers between 5 and 100.

MEG (SMP)

3 Put these numbers in order, smallest first.

3^2 $\quad$ 8^2 $\quad$ 2^3 $\quad$ 3^3 $\quad$ 5^2

4 Write 60 as a product of prime factors.

5 (a) Find the smallest number which is a multiple of 2, 3, 4 and 7.

(b) Find a square number other than one which is also a cube number.

6 Find the reciprocals of these numbers.

(a) 8 $\quad$ (b) 0·04 $\quad$ (c) 0·0005 $\quad$ (d) $\frac{1}{5}$ $\quad$ (e) $\frac{4}{9}$

7

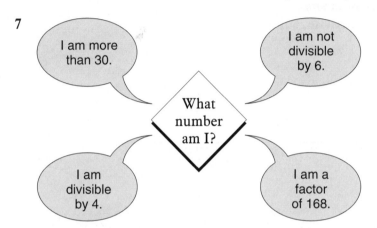

I am more than 30.

I am not divisible by 6.

What number am I?

I am divisible by 4.

I am a factor of 168.

8

20	21	22	23	24	25	26	27	28	29
30	31	32	33	34	35	36	37	38	39

From this list of numbers find

(a) a prime number

(b) a number which is **both** a multiple of 7 **and** a multiple of 5

(c) a cube number.

MEG (SMP)

9 (a) Sally makes a square patchwork quilt which has an area of 289 sq cm. How long are its sides?

(b) Sheena has 810 multilink cubes. What is the largest solid cube she could make from them?

10 (a) Harry is thinking of a number. It is a square number, a multiple of 12 and less than 100. What number is Harry thinking of?

(b) Helen is thinking of an odd number. It is a prime number and it is also a factor of 56. What number is Helen thinking of?

MEG (SMP)

Answers and hints ► page 104

Rounding

Rounding to the nearest ten, hundred, thousand, ...

4572 to the nearest hundred is 4600. ⟵ *4572 has been rounded up.*

48 231 to the nearest thousand is 48 000. ⟵ *48 231 has been rounded down.*

655 to the nearest ten is 660. ⟵ *655 has been rounded up.*

There is a simple rule for rounding whole numbers.
If the next figure is 5 or more, round up; otherwise round down.

Rounding to a number of decimal places

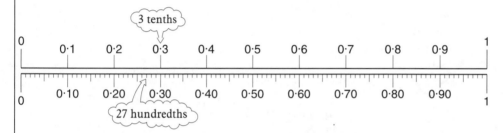

0·27 is nearer to 0·30 than to 0·20, so 0·27 = 0·3 to the nearest tenth.

We write   0·27 = 0·3 to 1 decimal place   or   0·27 = 0·3 to 1 d.p.

Measuring
► **page 58**

0·65 is exactly halfway between 0·60 and 0·70,
but we use the same rule for rounding and write   0·65 = 0·7 to 1 d.p.

Calculators often give long 'strings' of decimal places.

If you want to round this number to 2 decimal places,
you need to look at the figure in the 3rd decimal place.

7·32|78149 is rounded up to 7·33.

3rd decimal place

---

1 Round each of these to the nearest hundred.

(a) 6880   (b) 1076   (c) 26 207   (d) 951

2 Write these numbers in order of size, smallest first.

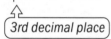 0·3   1·03   1   0·253   0·10

MEG (SMP)

3 Round each of these as described in the brackets.

(a) 0·55 (1 d.p.)   (b) 3·007 (2 d.p.)   (c) 16·48971 (3 d.p.)

4 An atlas gives the population of Paris as 10 073 000.
What is this population to the nearest million?   MEG (SMP)

5 Mrs Patel bought 25 square metres of carpet for her lounge.
It cost £18·75 a square metre.
How much did she pay? Give your answer to the nearest pound.

6 Tariq works $37\frac{1}{2}$ hours a week, for which he is paid £145·50.
What is his hourly rate?

7 It is claimed that in Florida there are eleven lightning strikes
every minute.

(a) How many is this in a day?

(b) How many is this in one year?
Give your answer in millions, correct to the nearest million.   MEG/ULEAC (SMP)

8 A tin of paint costs £10·79.
It contains 2·5 litres of paint.

(a) How much does the paint cost per litre?
(Give your answer to the nearest penny.)

One litre of paint should cover an area of about 14 m².

(b) What area should the paint in the tin cover?   MEG/ULEAC (SMP)

9 (a) Sally wants to change £600 into dollars for a trip to America.
The rate of exchange is $1·544 to £1.
How much (to the nearest dollar) will she receive?

(b) Tim brings back 200 marks from a holiday in Germany.
The bank buys marks at 2·384 marks to £1.
How much (to the nearest pound) will Tim get?

10 (a) Naheed buys £18 worth of petrol at a petrol station
selling petrol at 47·8p per litre.
Further along the road she notices another garage
selling petrol at 51·3p per litre.
How much more, to the nearest penny, would she have paid
for the same amount of petrol at this garage?

(b) There are approximately 4·55 litres in a gallon.
How many gallons of petrol has she bought?   WJEC

Answers and hints ► page 104

Significant figures

You may be asked to give an answer to a number of **significant figures**.

$31\,085 = 30\,000$ to 1 significant figure
$31\,085 = 31\,000$ to 2 significant figures
$31\,085 = 31\,100$ to 3 significant figures

Notice that $31{\cdot}085 = 31{\cdot}1$ to 3 s.f.

Rounding decimal numbers which lie between 0 and 1

You have to be careful to identify the first significant figure.
To do this, work from the decimal point to the right
until you reach the first non-zero figure.

$0{\cdot}007\,04 = 0{\cdot}007$ to 1 s.f.

This is the first significant figure.

$0{\cdot}007\,04 = 0{\cdot}0070$ to 2 s.f.

These two zeros must be included to keep the answer the correct size.

This zero is significant.

1 Round each of these as described.

  (a) $48\,560$ to 2 s.f.   (b) $0{\cdot}0348$ to 1 s.f.   (c) $58{\cdot}7$ to 2 s.f.

  (d) 1008 to 3 s.f.   (e) $0{\cdot}000\,706$ to 2 s.f.   (f) $0{\cdot}925$ to 1 s.f.

  (g) $489{\cdot}6$ to 3 s.f.   (h) $2{\cdot}086$ to 2 s.f.   (i) $0{\cdot}0503$ to 2 s.f.

2

43 000 ATTEND FOOTBALL MATCH

The actual attendance at this match was $42\,945$.
To how many significant figures does the newspaper headline
report the attendance?

3 1 metre of steel wire weighs $1{\cdot}74\,\text{kg}$.
   How much will 155 metres of wire weigh? Give your answer correct to 3 s.f.

4 1 gallon is approximately equal to $4{\cdot}55$ litres.
   An orange juice dispenser contains 35 litres.
   How many gallons is this? Give your answer correct to 2 s.f.

5 A pad of paper contains 250 sheets.
   The pad is $2{\cdot}6\,\text{cm}$ thick.
   What is the thickness of one sheet of paper?
   Give your answer in centimetres correct to 2 s.f.

Answers and hints ► page 105

Negative numbers

Adding a negative number does the same thing as
subtracting the equivalent positive number.
For example, $4 + {}^-2 = 4 - 2 = 2$ and ${}^-4 + {}^-2 = {}^-4 - 2 = {}^-6$.

Subtracting a negative number does the same thing as
adding the equivalent positive number.
For example, $4 - {}^-2 = 4 + 2 = 6$ and ${}^-4 - {}^-2 = {}^-4 + 2 = {}^-2$.

This table shows the rules for the signs when
you multiply or divide positive and negative numbers.
For example, $3 \times {}^-4 = {}^-12$ and ${}^-12 \div {}^-3 = 4$.

		Second number	
$\times$ or $\div$		pos	neg
First	pos	pos	neg
number	neg	neg	pos

1   The minimum temperatures, in degrees Celsius, for the first
    seven days in January were

          2      ${}^-5$ ${}^-1$ 0 ${}^-3$ 4   3

    Write these temperatures in order of size with the lowest first.   MEG (SMP)

2   Work out these.
    (a) ${}^-6 + {}^-7$ (b) $3 - {}^-8$ (c) ${}^-4 \times {}^-5$ (d) $5 \div {}^-2$
    (e) ${}^-8 \div {}^-4$ (f) $\frac{1}{2} \times {}^-12$ (g) ${}^-0.2 \times 5$ (h) ${}^-14 \div 3.5$

3   On a December day the temperature in London was ${}^-3°$C.
    (a) In Paris it was $7°$ warmer.
        What was the temperature in Paris?
    (b) In Moscow it was $7°$ colder than in London.
        What was the temperature in Moscow?   MEG (SMP)

4   An air temperature below ${}^-13°$C can be dangerous to
    light aircraft. It can produce severe freezing.
    (a) The air temperature on the ground is $17°$C.
        How many $°$C is this above the dangerous temperature?
    (b) Air temperature **falls** by $1°$C for every 100m rise in height.
        If the air temperature on the ground is $12°$C, what is the
        greatest height the light plane can safely fly at without
        danger of freezing?   MEG (SMP)

5   The highest point in the United States of America is the
    summit of Mount McKinley at $20\,270$ feet above sea level.
    The lowest point is in Death Valley at 280 feet below sea level.
    What is the difference in height between these two points?   MEG/ULEAC (SMP)

Answers and hints ► page 106

Fractions

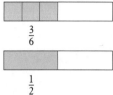

$\frac{3}{6}$ is equal to $\frac{1}{2}$.

$\frac{3}{6}$

$\frac{1}{2}$

$\frac{1}{2}$ and $\frac{3}{6}$ are called **equivalent fractions**. *Notice that* $\frac{1}{2}$ $\overset{\times 3}{\underset{\times 3}{\rightleftarrows}}$ $\frac{3}{6}$.

To **add** or **subtract** fractions, arrange for them to have the same bottom number.
We use equivalent fractions to do this.

Example 1 $\frac{2}{3} + \frac{1}{12} = \frac{2 \times 4}{3 \times 4} + \frac{1}{12}$ *Multiply the top and bottom numbers of* $\frac{2}{3}$ *by 4.*

$$= \frac{8}{12} + \frac{1}{12}$$

$$= \frac{9}{12} = \frac{9 \div 3}{12 \div 3}$$ *Divide the top and bottom numbers by 3 to* **simplify** *the fraction (put it in its* **lowest terms**).

$$= \frac{3}{4}$$

Example 2 $\frac{3}{8} - \frac{1}{3} = \frac{3 \times 3}{8 \times 3} - \frac{1 \times 8}{3 \times 8} = \frac{9}{24} - \frac{8}{24} = \frac{1}{24}$

To **multiply** fractions, multiply together the top numbers to get the top number
and multiply together the bottom numbers to get the bottom number. For example:

$$\frac{2}{3} \times \frac{1}{4} = \frac{2 \times 1}{3 \times 4} = \frac{2}{12} = \frac{1}{6}$$ *Divide the top and bottom numbers by 2 to simplify the fraction.*

To **divide** by a fraction, for example to work out $20 \div \frac{1}{4}$, we need to find
how many quarters are in 20.

Reciprocals
► page 2

(Since there are 4 quarters in 1 the answer must be $20 \times 4 = 80$.)

Here are some more examples:

How many $\frac{1}{8}$s in 5?   How many $\frac{1}{8}$s in $\frac{3}{4}$?   How many $\frac{2}{3}$s in $\frac{7}{8}$?

$5 \div \frac{1}{8} = 5 \times 8 = 40$ $\frac{3}{4} \div \frac{1}{8} = \frac{3}{4} \times 8 = \frac{24}{4} = 6$ $\frac{7}{8} \div \frac{2}{3} = \frac{7}{8} \times \frac{3}{2} = \frac{21}{16}$

We can write a 'top-heavy' fraction as a **mixed number**: $\frac{21}{16} = \frac{16 + 5}{16} = 1 + \frac{5}{16} = 1\frac{5}{16}$

1 Work out these. Give your answers in their simplest form.

   (a) $\frac{3}{8} + \frac{3}{4}$ (b) $\frac{2}{5} - \frac{1}{4}$ (c) $1\frac{7}{8} - \frac{3}{4}$ (d) $\frac{1}{2} + \frac{2}{3} + \frac{3}{4}$

   (e) $\frac{3}{4} \times \frac{1}{2}$ (f) $\frac{7}{8} \div 2$ (g) $\frac{5}{6} \times \frac{2}{3}$ (h) $\frac{2}{5} \div \frac{1}{3}$

2 Work out these.

   (a) $\frac{1}{3} \times £24$ (b) $\frac{2}{3} \times 30\,\text{cm}$ (c) $\frac{3}{4} \times 12$ inches

3 Would you rather have $\frac{1}{4}$ of £50 or $\frac{3}{8}$ of £24?
Show your working.

4

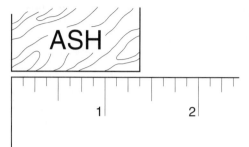 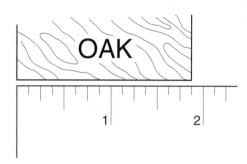

Megan measures the thickness of the two pieces of wood in inches.
The diagrams show the pieces of wood measured.

(a) Write down the thickness of each piece.

(b) She puts the two pieces together. She needs an extra piece to
make the total thickness $3\frac{1}{2}$ inches.

What is the thickness of the extra piece Megan needs?

WJEC

5 A shopkeeper sold 45 Topaz bars from a full box of 120 bars.

(a) What fraction did he sell?
Give the answer in its simplest form.

(b) Of the 45 bars sold, $\frac{2}{3}$ were bought by children.
How many bars did the children buy?

MEG/ULEAC (SMP)

6 The Saddlethorpe Cricket Club give a
trophy for the best player each season.

The trophy is $6\frac{3}{4}$ inches high.

It stands on a base $1\frac{5}{8}$ inches high.

What is the total height of the trophy and base?

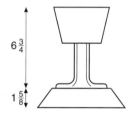

MEG/ULEAC (SMP)

7 'SEMPEL' is an aftershave. The original bottles held 250 ml
and were sold for £1·89.

To encourage sales, a larger bottle has been produced.
It contains $\frac{1}{3}$ more aftershave but costs only $\frac{2}{3}$ of the
price of the original bottle.

(a) What is the price of the larger bottle?

(b) How much does the larger bottle hold?

$\frac{1}{3}$ more for
$\frac{2}{3}$ of the price

MEG/ULEAC (SMP)

Answers and hints ► page 106

Fractions, decimals and percentages

Converting between fractions, decimals and percentages

This diagram shows that
30% of cheddar cheese is fat.

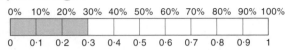

You can see that 30% = 0·3.
You can work it out this way.

$$30\% = \frac{30}{100} = 30 \div 100 = 0.3$$

Divide the percentage by 100 to get a fraction. *Do the division to get a decimal.*

This diagram shows that 85% of butter is fat.
We can convert the decimal like this:

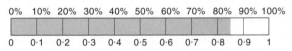

$0.85 = 0.85 \times 100\% = 85\%$ *Multiply by 100 to change the decimal to a percentage.*

Expressing one quantity as a percentage of another

There are 55 g of fat in a piece of beef weighing 275 g.
The fraction of fat in beef is $\frac{55}{275}$.

$\frac{55}{275} = 55 \div 275 = 0.2$ *Change the fraction to a decimal.*

$0.2 = 0.2 \times 100\% = 20\%$ *Multiply by 100 to change the decimal to a percentage.*

So 20% of the beef is fat.

1   Write these as decimals.
   (a) 16%   (b) $\frac{75}{100}$ (c) 0·1%   (d) $\frac{1}{16}$

2   Write these as percentages.
   (a) 0·81   (b) $\frac{3}{8}$ (c) 0·725   (d) $\frac{17}{25}$

3   Write each of these as a fraction in its simplest form.
   (a) 45%   (b) 0·9   (c) 0·66   (d) 34%

4   Work out these in your head.
   (a) 25% of 64 kg   (b) 5% of £10   (c) 20% of £1·50   (d) 75% of 20 m

5   Put these fractions in order, from the smallest to the largest.
   $$\frac{7}{8} \qquad \frac{3}{5} \qquad \frac{5}{6} \qquad \frac{2}{3} \qquad \frac{5}{7}$$

   Show your working. You may use a calculator if you wish.   MEG/ULEAC (SMP)

6 80 students applied to go on an outward-bound course.
Three-fifths of them were boys.

(a) How many boys applied?

(b) 56 students were accepted on the course.
What percentage of the number who applied is this?

7 Work out each of these in your head.

(a) 9 as a percentage of 36   (b) £3 as a percentage of £25

(c) 15 g as a percentage of 1000 g   (d) 25p as a percentage of £2

8 In a sale the price of a CD player was reduced from £150 to £126.
Find the discount as a percentage of the original price.   WJEC

9 In a local election, $\frac{3}{5}$ of the electorate voted.

The Green Party received $\frac{1}{4}$ of the votes cast.

(a) What percentage of the electorate voted?

(b) What percentage of the electorate voted for the Green Party?

(c) What percentage of the electorate did **not** vote for the Green Party?

10 The table shows the type of bacon
preferred by the 500 people questioned.

(a) Copy and complete the table.

(b) Use it to find the percentage of people
who preferred smoked bacon.

	streaky	middle	back	TOTAL
smoked	15			
unsmoked		126	195	
TOTAL	60	150		500

11 The town of Brackhurst has a population of 46 000.
28% of the population are children and 16 100 are women.

(a) How many children live in Brackhurst?

(b) (i) What percentage of the population are women?
    (ii) What percentage of the population are men?   MEG

12 Mr and Mrs Griffiths want to move house.
An estate agent advertises their house at an asking price of £48 000.
The house is eventually sold for £42 000.

(a) Calculate the percentage by which Mr and Mrs Griffiths
reduced their asking price.

(b) The estate agent charges a fee of $1\frac{1}{2}$% of the selling price of the house.
Calculate the amount they pay the estate agent.   WJEC

Answers and hints ► page 107

Percentages

Finding a value after a percentage increase or decrease

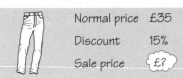

Hire charge	£120
VAT rate	17·5%
Total cost	£?

Total cost = 117·5% of hire charge (that is 100% + 17·5%)
= £120 × 1·175   *The multiplying factor is 1·175.*
= £141

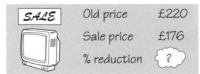

Normal price	£35
Discount	15%
Sale price	£?

Sale price = 85% of normal price (that is 100% − 15%)
= £35 × 0·85   *The multiplying factor is 0·85.*
= £29·75

Finding a percentage increase or decrease

Old price	£220
Sale price	£176
% reduction	?

There are two ways of doing this:

Work out the increase or decrease.

Decrease = £220 − £176 = £44

Percentage decrease = $\dfrac{\text{decrease}}{\text{old price}} \times 100\%$

$= \dfrac{44}{220} \times 100\% = 20\%$

or

Write the fraction $\dfrac{\text{new price}}{\text{old price}}$ and change it to a percentage.

$\dfrac{176}{220} = 0\cdot8 = 80\%$

The new price is 80% of the old price.

The percentage decrease is 100% − 80% = 20%.

Compound percentages

Example
£500 is invested for two years.

In the first year the interest rate is 5%. In the second year it is 4%.

How much money is in the account after 2 years?

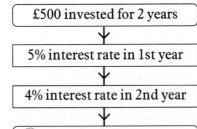

£500 invested for 2 years
↓
5% interest rate in 1st year
↓
4% interest rate in 2nd year
↓
£? in account after 2 years

Total after 1 year
= £500 × 1·05

Total after 2 years
= (total after 1 year) × 1·04
= £500 × 1·05 × 1·04
= £546

Percentages backwards

Old price	?
% increase	12%
New price	£140

Old price × 1·12 = £140 (new price)

Old price = $\dfrac{£140}{1\cdot12} = £125$ *Divide both sides of the equation by 1·12.*

1 A decorator charges £190 plus VAT to decorate a room.
The VAT rate is 17·5%.
How much VAT does he add to the bill?

WJEC

2 (a) Find the sale price of a sweater marked at £24·50.
(b) You buy a coat in the sale for £42.
Work out the price before it was reduced.

> **SALE**
> **20% off all**
> **marked prices**

3 On Saturday at noon a population of bacteria is estimated at 3000.
If the population increases by 10% every 24 hours, what will it be
at noon on the following Monday?

4 The number of pupils at Swinburn School is 4% more this year than last.
This year there are 988 pupils. How many pupils were there last year?

5 In 1995 the number of visitors to a theme park was 680000.
The next year the number of visitors was 755000.
What percentage increase was this?

6 When Mr Lee started work his **gross** salary (salary before deductions) was £6400.
His personal allowance (on which he paid no tax) was £2425.
He paid 25% tax on his taxable pay.
(a) On what sum did he pay income tax?
(b) Calculate how much tax he paid.

Mr Lee also paid 7% national insurance on his gross salary.
(c) Calculate how much national insurance he paid.
(d) What were his total deductions?
(e) What was his **net** monthly income (income after deductions)?

7 In a country suffering from high inflation, the cost of petrol rose
by 15% one month and by a further 20% the following month.
What was the overall percentage increase for the two months?

MEG (SMP)

8 To encourage careful driving, insurance companies
offer discounts to drivers who make no accident claims.

1 year's no claims discount	15%
2 years' no claims discount	25%
3 years' no claims discount	35%
4 years' no claims discount	50%

(a) The full premium for insuring Ian's car is £460,
but he has 1 year's no claims discount.
Use the table to find how much he will have to pay.
(b) Lisa has 3 years' no claims discount.
She pays a premium of £163·80.
What would her premium have been without her discount?

Answers and hints ► page 107

Ratio and proportion

Simplest form

The **ratio** of black squares to white squares
in each of these diagrams is 1 to 2 or 1:2.

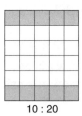

1:2 is the **simplest form** of the ratios 3:6 and 10:20.
We say that these three ratios are **equivalent**.

Sharing in a given ratio

To share £200 in the ratio 2:3, divide £200 into $2 + 3 = 5$ equal parts.
$\frac{1}{5}$ of £200 = £40.

So the shares of the money will be $2 \times £40 = £80$ and $3 \times £40 = £120$.

Remember to check by adding the shares: $80 + 120 = 200$.

Proportional quantities and their graphs

Graphs and proportion
► page 38

The table shows the amount of calcium in various amounts of milk.
If this data is plotted, the graph is a straight line passing through $(0, 0)$.
Any two quantities which are related in this way are said to be
proportional.

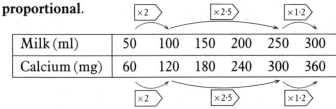

Milk (ml)	50	100	150	200	250	300
Calcium (mg)	60	120	180	240	300	360

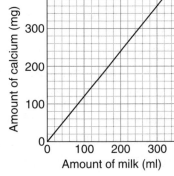

Notice how the quantities in the table are related.

Suppose you wanted to find out how much calcium there is in
half a pint of milk (1 pint = 568 millilitres).

You could either read the answer from the graph or *calculate* using one of these two methods.

Multiplier method for calculating proportion

When you multiply one quantity by a number, you need to
multiply the other quantity by the same number.

$50\,\text{ml}$ $\times?$ $284\,\text{ml}$
$60\,\text{mg}$ $\times?$ $?\,\text{mg}$ *Multiplier*

Divide 284 by 50 to get the **multiplier** 5·68.

So the amount of calcium in 284 ml = $60 \times 5 \cdot 68\,\text{mg} = 341\,\text{mg}$ (to the nearest mg).

Unitary method for calculating proportion

50 ml   contains   60 mg.

÷50   ÷50   *Divide by 50 to find the amount of calcium in 1 ml.*

1 ml   contains $\frac{60}{50}$ mg.

×284   ×284   *Multiply by 284 to find the amount of calcium in 284 ml.*

284 ml   contains $\frac{60}{50} \times 284\,\text{mg} = 341\,\text{mg}$ (to the nearest mg).

1 Write these ratios in their simplest form.

   (a) 4:12   (b) 20:5   (c) 2·2:3·3   (d) 10:24

   (e) 15:18   (f) $3\frac{1}{2}$:5   (g) 15p:£1   (h) 1 hour:15 minutes

2 Miss Parker and Mrs Hanif invested a total of £120000 in a new business.
   Miss Parker and Mrs Hanif invested their money in the ratio of 5:3.

   (a) How much did Mrs Hanif invest?

   (b) They agreed that the profit should be shared in the same ratio as their investments.
       In the first year Miss Parker received £14500 as her share of the profit.
       How much profit did the business make in the first year?   MEG (SMP)

3 A 30cm ruler is cut into two pieces as shown.
   The 12cm piece weighs 8 grams.
   Work out the weight of the 18cm piece.

   MEG (SMP)

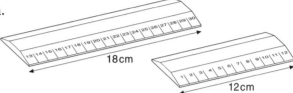

4 Bronze is a mixture of copper and tin. The copper and
   tin are mixed in the ratio 9:1 by weight.

   (a) How much tin is there in a bronze brooch weighing 270g?

   (b) Another bronze brooch contains 180g of copper.
       How much does it weigh altogether?   MEG

5 Three house owners agree to tarmac the road outside their houses at a
   total cost of £5600.
   The lengths of road in front of their houses are 27m, 34·5m and 18·5m.
   They decide to share the payment in the same ratio as these lengths.
   Calculate the largest of the payments.   WJEC

6 The ratio of the volume of oil to the volume of vinegar in French dressing
   for salads is 5:2.

   (a) How much oil must be added to 300ml of vinegar to make some French dressing?

   (b) A chef needs a litre of the French dressing.
       Calculate the volumes of oil and vinegar needed.
       Give your answers to the nearest 10ml.   WJEC

7 A chain-saw instruction booklet states:

   The engine is lubricated by oil in the fuel mixture.
   Mixture ratio 1 to 25.

   This mixture ratio usually means the ratio of oil to petrol.
   However, what is the ratio of oil to petrol in
   the accompanying diagram?
   Give your answer in the form 1 to n.   MEG (SMP)

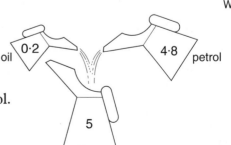

Answers and hints ► page 108

Estimation, checking and accuracy

Checking using an inverse operation

You can check a subtraction by adding.

$$\begin{array}{r} 184 \\ -115 \\ \hline 69 \end{array}$$ $\boxed{115 + 69 = 184}$

You can check a division by multiplying.

$$165 \div 11 = 15 \quad \boxed{15 \times 11 = 165}$$

Checking by rounding

This is useful for making sure your answer is about the right size when you are using a calculator. For example:

$$28{\cdot}7 + (6{\cdot}3 \times 8{\cdot}8) \approx 30 + (6 \times 9) = 84$$

$$580 \div 0{\cdot}6 \approx 600 \div 0{\cdot}6 = 1000$$

$$\frac{910 \times 0{\cdot}9}{23} \approx \frac{900 \times 1}{20} = 45$$

Rounding ► page 4

Significant figures ► page 6

Make sure you can use your calculator to do calculations like these:

(a) $50 - (8 \times 4)$ (b) $\dfrac{20}{2 \times 2{\cdot}5}$ (c) $100 - \dfrac{90}{30}$

You will need to use the memory and/or bracket keys on your calculator. Check by working them out in your head.

[The answers you should get are: (a) 18   (b) 4   (c) 97]

You should also be able to use your calculator efficiently to cope with 'constant' functions, for example $12 \times 1{\cdot}25, \ 15 \times 1{\cdot}25, \ 24 \times 1{\cdot}25$.

---

1   Qasim calculated that $\frac{4780}{275} = 17{\cdot}38$.

    Use estimation without a calculator to check whether
    this is approximately correct.
    Show your method clearly, writing down the approximations
    you make.

MEG/ULEAC (SMP)

2   Jasbir is buying bags of sand.
    She needs 19 bags.
    Each bag costs £3·78.

    Write down a calculation that
    you could do in your head
    to **estimate** the cost of the sand.

MEG (SMP)

3 Show clearly how you would obtain an **estimate** for the following calculation.

$$(860 \times 0.28) \div (89 \div 3.13)$$

4 Use a calculator to work out:

(a) $\dfrac{46.64 - 26.12}{4.56}$ (b) $7 \times (9.84 - 0.07)$ (c) $\dfrac{3.162}{0.04 \times 5.1}$

Check the size of your answers by rounding the numbers in each calculation.

5 Do these on your calculator. Give each answer correct to 1 d.p.

(a) $8.76 - (4.2 \times 3.1)$ (b) $\dfrac{85}{1.2 - 0.65}$ (c) $\dfrac{3.2^2 - 0.81^2}{3 \times 0.7}$

Check your answers by rounding.

6 (a) Convert 280 miles to kilometres (1 km ≈ 0.62 miles).

(b) A 15 kg bag of potatoes costs £7. What is the cost per kilogram?

(c) Convert $220 to pounds sterling assuming an exchange rate of $1.544 to £1.

Give each answer to a suitable degree of accuracy and state what it is.

7 (a) Imagine your calculator has broken. You have to find the result of

$$435 \div 17$$

correct to one decimal place. Show your working.

(b) What simpler calculation (that you can do in your head) could you do to check the answer to (a)? Write down the calculation and the result.   MEG/ULEAC (SMP)

8 Miss Sondh drove 644 miles on her holiday. She used 74 litres of petrol. She wanted to estimate how many miles she could drive on one litre.

(a) Write down suitable approximate values for the distance she drove and the petrol used.

(b) Use these figures to find mentally an estimate of how many miles she drove on one litre.   MEG/ULEAC (SMP)

9 Bob spilled tomato ketchup on his homework, so that some of the digits cannot be read.

(1) ▮59 × 57 = 18▮55

(2) ▮42 + 6▮6 = 1▮78

(3) 6▮2 ÷ 0.3▮ = 0.0173▮

Only one of his answers could be correct. The other two must be wrong.

(a) Which of his three answers **could** be correct?

(b) For **each** of the other **two** answers, say why it **must** be wrong.   WJEC

Answers and hints ► page 109

Indices

Numbers such as 1000 and 1 million can be written as **powers** of ten. For example:

$$1000 = 10 \times 10 \times 10 = 10^3 \text{ (10 to the power of 3)}$$

$$1\,000\,000 = 10 \times 10 \times 10 \times 10 \times 10 \times 10 = 10^6 \text{ (10 to the power of 6)}$$

If we continue the pattern of powers to the right
of the decimal point, the powers become negative.

We use 10^{-1} to mean **1 tenth,**
10^{-2} to mean **1 hundredth**, and so on.

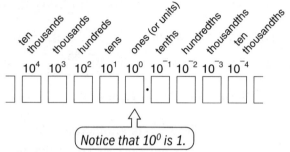

Notice that 10^0 is 1.

Powers of ten are useful for expressing large and small numbers. For example:

To find the index, count left
from the decimal point.

6 places

$$7\,600\,000 = 7 \cdot 6 \text{ million} = 7 \cdot 6 \times 10^6$$

$7 \cdot 6 \times 10^6$ is called the **standard index form** of $7\,600\,000$.
Note that the first part has to be a number between 1 and 10.

4 places

Similarly, $0 \cdot 000\,55 = 5 \cdot 5 \times 10^{-4}$.

To find the index, count right from the decimal point.

Make sure you can use the
exponent key on your
calculator to handle
numbers in standard
index form.

Simplifying expressions involving indices

The rules of
indices ► page 27

To multiply you **add** the indices. $\quad 5^2 \times 5^4 = (5 \times 5) \times (5 \times 5 \times 5 \times 5) = 5^6$

$$10^6 \div 10^2 = \frac{10 \times 10 \times 10 \times 10 \times 10 \times 10}{10 \times 10} = 10^4$$

To divide you **subtract** the indices.

$$2^2 \div 2^5 = \frac{2 \times 2}{2 \times 2 \times 2 \times 2 \times 2} = \frac{1}{2^3} = 2^{-3}$$

1 Convert these numbers to ordinary form.
   (a) $8 \cdot 1 \times 10^5$ (b) $6 \cdot 5 \times 10^4$ (c) 7×10^8

2 Write these numbers in standard index form.
   (a) $417\,000$ (b) $0 \cdot 000\,000\,217$ (c) $0 \cdot 003\,04$ (d) $60\,000\,000$

3 Simplify these. Write your answers using index notation.

(a) $6^3 \times 6^2$ (b) $2^8 \div 2^3$ (c) $10^2 \times 10^2 \times 10^2$

(d) $(10^2)^3$ (e) $10^6 \div 10^4$ (f) $9 \div 3^4$

(g) $2^3 \div 2^0$ (h) $5^4 \times 5$ (i) $a^6 \div a^2$

4 Use the power key on your calculator to evaluate these.

(a) 4^5 (b) 5^6 (c) $0{\cdot}3^5$ (d) 2^{10}

5 (a) Write $0{\cdot}007$ in standard form.

(b) Explain, without using a calculator, how you can tell that the following calculation must be wrong.

$$(4{\cdot}1 \times 10^7) \times (3{\cdot}9 \times 10^{17}) = 1{\cdot}599 \times 10^{24}$$

MEG (SMP)

6 Dinosaurs died out about 66 million years ago.
They first appeared on Earth 280 million years ago.

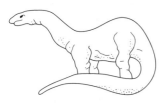

For roughly how many years did they exist?
Give your answer in standard index form

MEG/ULEAC (SMP)

7 (a) Write each of the following numbers in standard form.

(i) $93\,000\,000$ (ii) $0{\cdot}000\,14$

(b) Find, in standard form, the value of:

(i) $(6{\cdot}7 \times 10^{-5}) \times (8{\cdot}3 \times 10^{12})$ (ii) $(3{\cdot}4 \times 10^{-2}) \div (8{\cdot}84 \times 10^3)$

WJEC

8 The Sultan of Brunei is believed to be the richest man in the world.
His income is said to be $225\,000$ every hour.
How much is his income in a year?
Give your answer in standard index form to 2 significant figures.

MEG/ULEAC (SMP)

9 What is the difference in value between $8{\cdot}7 \times 10^5$ and $8{\cdot}7^5$?
Give your answer to 4 significant figures.

MEG/ULEAC (SMP)

10 1 megawatt $= 1\,000\,000$ watts.
1 terawatt $= 1\,000\,000\,000\,000$ watts.

(a) The biggest laser in the world has a power of 51 terawatts.
How many watts is this? Give your answer in standard form.

(b) All the power stations in the UK, working together, can produce a power of $6{\cdot}5 \times 10^{-2}$ terawatts.
How many megawatts is this?

MEG

Answers and hints ▶ page 110

Mixed number

1   A packet of McVitie's 'normal' Digestive biscuits
    contains 22·1 g of fat per 100 g of biscuits.

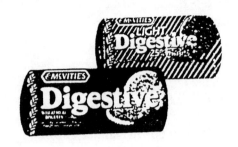

(a) How much fat does a 450 g packet of 'normal'
    Digestive biscuits contain?

Light Digestive biscuits contain 25% less fat than
'normal' digestive biscuits.

(b) How much fat does a 450 g packet of
    Light Digestive biscuits contain?

MEG/ULEAC (SMP)

2   The total cost of a pizza is £2·50.
    This diagram shows how the £2·50 is made up.

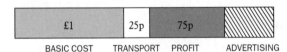

£1	25p	75p	

BASIC COST   TRANSPORT PROFIT   ADVERTISING

(a) How much of the pizza's cost is spent on advertising?

(b) (i)   What fraction of the total cost is profit?
    (ii) Write this fraction as a decimal.
    (iii) What percentage of the total cost is profit?

WJEC

3   The table below shows the rooms available each night and the
    charges at the Crown Hotel.

	Double room (for 2 people)	Single room (for 1 person)
Number of rooms available	78	42
Charge for each room	£83	£54

(a) Calculate the greatest number of people the hotel can accommodate
    each night.

On one particular night, 56 double rooms and 34 single rooms were occupied.

(b) (i)   Express the total number of rooms occupied as a fraction of
          the total number of rooms available at the hotel.
          Give the fraction in its simplest form.
    (ii) Calculate the total charge for the rooms which were occupied.
    (iii) Express the number of people accommodated on this night
          as a percentage of the greatest number the hotel can accommodate.
          Give your answer correct to 3 significant figures.

MEG

4   The rule for this sequence is 'Add the next prime number'.

        5   7   10   15   ...   ...

    Write down the next two numbers in the sequence.

5 A light year is the distance travelled by light in one year, approximately 9 500 000 000 000 km.

(a) Express the number of kilometres in one light year in standard form.

The star, Proxima Centauri, is 4·3 light years away from the Earth.

(b) Calculate the distance, in km, from Proxima Centauri to the Earth. Give your answer in standard form.

The Sun is approximately 150 000 000 km from the Earth.

(c) How many times further from the Earth is Proxima Centauri than the Sun?

ULEAC

6 (a) Calculate the value of 4^3.

(b) Calculate the value of 4^{-3}.

(c) Find the smallest whole number value of n for which

4^n is greater than 1000.

ULEAC

7 In 1993 the total entry for a particular examination was 151 828 candidates. In 1994 it was estimated that the total entry for the same examination would be 95 000 candidates.

(a) Calculate the percentage decrease in the number of candidates from 1993 to 1994.

Each candidate sits two examination papers. Each examiner marks about 500 papers.
The examination board calculated that it required 650 examiners **in 1993**.

(b) Write down a calculation you can do in your head to check this number. Comment on the result.

MEG (SMP)

8 A shop sells a pack of 3 tumblers for £2·99. It also sells a pack of 8 tumblers for £6·99.

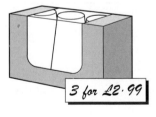

3 for £2·99

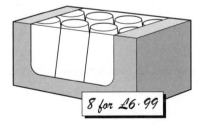

8 for £6·99

(a) Which pack gives the better value for money? Show your working clearly.

(b) Why might someone buy the pack that does not give the better value for money?

MEG (SMP)

Answers and hints ► page 111

ALGEBRA
Simplifying and substituting

Adding and subtracting like terms

These are **like terms** (they are amounts of the same number, a). Whatever the value of a, (3 lots of a) + (4 lots of a) gives 7 lots of a.

You can't combine $7c$ with anything in this expression (for example, $2b$ and $7c$ are not like terms).

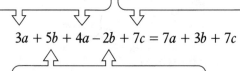

$$3a + 5b + 4a - 2b + 7c = 7a + 3b + 7c$$

These are **like terms** because both are amounts of b. (5 lots of b) – (2 lots of b) gives 3 lots of b.

Make sure you agree that terms have been combined correctly in these.

$$c + c^2 + c = c^2 + 2c$$

$$ab + 6b + 2ab - 2b = 3ab + 4b$$

---

1 Simplify these algebraic expressions, where possible.

(a) $a + a + 2a + a$ (b) $4d - d + 2$ (c) $n^2 + 2n$

(d) $ef + fe + f + e$ (e) $4c + 3d + 7c + 8d$ (f) $5a - 6b - 3a + 8b$

(g) $p + 2q + r - q + 2r$ (h) $3m + 2mn + 2n - mn$ (i) $3g - 2h - 4g + h$

Multiplying

$3a \times 4b$ can be written out as $3 \times a \times 4 \times b$.

You can do multiplications in any order, so the expression becomes $3 \times 4 \times a \times b$, which simplifies to $12ab$.

Make sure you understand how these have been done.

$$6ab \times 3c^2 = 18abc^2$$

$$2a \times 5ba = 10a^2b$$

Indices ► page 18

The rules of indices ► page 27

---

2 Simplify each of these expressions.

(a) $2a \times 6a$ (b) $ab \times a$ (c) $2ab \times 5a$ (d) $2xy \times 2yx$

(e) $ac \times ab$ (f) $3a^2 \times 2ab$ (g) $4x^2 \times xy^2$ (h) $\frac{1}{2}ab^2 \times 6ac^2$

Dividing

You can write a division in the form of a fraction: $3ab \div 7a = \dfrac{3ab}{7}$

When you divide the top and bottom
of a fraction by the same number
the result stays the same.

$$\frac{3ab}{7a} \xrightarrow{\ \div a\ } \frac{3b}{7}$$

Make sure you understand how these have been done.

$$\frac{a^3 b}{ab} = a^2 \qquad \frac{2ab^4}{6b^2 c^3} = \frac{ab^2}{3c^3}$$

3 Simplify these expressions by dividing the top and bottom by the same number.

(a) $\dfrac{x^3}{x^2}$ (b) $\dfrac{3x^2 y^2}{5xy}$ (c) $\dfrac{4x^3 y}{2xy^3}$ (d) $\dfrac{ac^3}{a^2 b^2}$

Removing brackets

Brackets and factors
► page 27

Brackets can show that some operation outside the brackets applies to
all the numbers or terms inside the brackets.
For example, in the expression $2(x + 4)$ the 2 on the left means
multiply the x and the 4 by 2.
So $2(x + 4)$ is the same as $2 \times x + 2 \times 4$, that is $2x + 8$.

Make sure you understand how these have been done.

$$3a + 2(a - 6) = 3a + 2a - 12, \text{ which simplifies to } 5a - 12.$$
$$3a - 3(a - 6) = 3a - 3a + 18, \text{ which simplifies to } 18.$$
$$a^2 - 2a(a + b) = a^2 - 2a^2 - 2ab, \text{ which simplifies to } {}^-a^2 - 2ab.$$

4 Remove the brackets from these expressions and simplify them where possible.

(a) $2x + 3(y + 5)$ (b) $4c - 3(d - c)$ (c) $5a - (b - a)$

(d) $2y(y - 5)$ (e) $x^2 + x(x - 7)$ (f) ${}^-a^2 - 5a(a + 8)$

(g) $6 - a(3 - 2a)$ (h) ${}^-b^2 + 6b(b - 2)$ (i) $x(x + 3) + 3(x - 4)$

Substituting numbers into an expression

Negative numbers
► page 7

Be particularly careful with negative numbers.
For example, if $a = {}^-4$,

$$a^2 - 3(a - 2) = ({}^-4)^2 - 3({}^-4 - 2) = 16 - 3({}^-6) = 16 + 18 = 34$$

5 If $a = 3, b = {}^-5$ and $c = 10$, work out the values of these expressions.

(a) $a + b - c$ (b) $a^2 + b^2$ (c) $3a - 4b$ (d) $b(a + c)$

(e) $a + \dfrac{c}{b}$ (f) $\dfrac{c - b}{b}$ (g) $3a^2$ (h) $(3a)^2$

(i) $\frac{1}{2}(a + b)$ (j) ${}^-2c^2$ (k) $\frac{1}{2}c - b$ (l) $\frac{{}^-3}{4}(c - 2a)$

Answers and hints ► page 112

grad = up / atng

grad ÷ up

intercept

grad 2

eg. grad 3 = 3/1

grad −4 = −4/1

grad 2/3

Equations of straight line graphs

The graph of any equation in the form $y = mx + c$, where m and c are particular numbers, is always a straight line.

You only *need* to plot two points to be able to draw a straight line, but it is a good idea to check by plotting a third.
In the graph on the right we

- chose x-values of 0 and 2 which gave coordinates $(0, 1)$ and $(2, 5)$; it is sensible not to use points which are close together.

- checked that $(^-2, ^-3)$ on the line satisfied the equation $y = 2x + 1$ $\quad (^-3 = (2 \times ^-2) + 1 = ^-3)$.

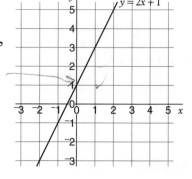

The measure of slope of a line is called its **gradient**.
It may be positive or negative, and can be calculated

from the fraction $\dfrac{\text{vertical change}}{\text{horizontal change}}$.

Gradients
► **pages 38, 62**

For an equation in the form $y = mx + c$,
the value of m gives the gradient and
c gives the value of y where the line
cuts the y-axis.

So if the line has a gradient of 2 and
cuts the y-axis at the point $(0, 1)$,
its equation is $y = 2x + 1$.

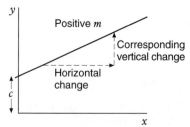

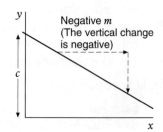

You could be asked to draw a line with an equation like $2x + 3y = 12$.
In an equation like this, where x and y are on the same side of the equation,
it is always sensible to try to find the points where the line
crosses the x- and y-axes.

Substituting 0 for x in $2x + 3y = 12$ gives $0 + 3y = 12$.
Solving this gives $y = 4$, so $(0, 4)$ is a point on the line.

Substituting 0 for y in $2x + 3y = 12$ gives $2x + 0 = 12$.
Solving this gives $x = 6$, so $(6, 0)$ is a point on the line.

Check that you agree that the gradient of $2x + 3y = 12$ is $\frac{^-2}{3}$.

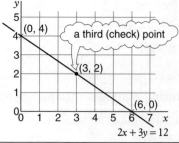

a third (check) point

1 Draw each pair of lines on a separate grid.
   (Use the same axes as at the top of the page but use 1 cm for each unit.)
   (a) $x = 1$ and $x = 4$ (b) $y = 3$ and $y = ^-2$
   (c) $y = x + 1$ and $y = x + 3$ (d) $y = 2x$ and $y = 2x - 3$

2 (a) Draw these lines on the same grid.
   (Use x-coordinates from $^-3$ to 6 and y-coordinates from $^-8$ to 8.)
   (i) $y = 3x - 1$ (ii) $2y = 3x + 4$ (iii) $3x - 2y = 6$
   (b) What is the gradient of each line?

$3x - 6 = 2y$
$1.5x - 3 = y$

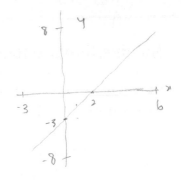

3 Which of the following points lie on the straight line whose equation is $4x - 5y = 4$?
   (a) $(6, 4)$ (b) $(1, 0)$ (c) $(0, 0)$ (d) $(4, 6)$ (e) $(^-4, ^-4)$

4 (a) Draw a line which passes through the points $(0, 2)$ and $(3, 5)$.
   (b) Where does it cut the y-axis?
   (c) Write down the equation of the line.

5 Write down the equations of the lines A, B, C and D
   in the graph below.

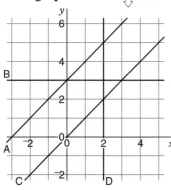 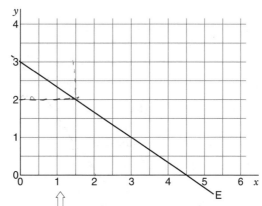

6 (a) Write down the equation of the line E above in the form $y = mx + c$.
   (b) Write down the equation of the line which is parallel to this line
       and passes through the point $(0, 6)$.

7 (a) Draw the line joining the points $(4, ^-1)$ and $(^-2, 2)$.
   (b) What is the equation of this line?

MEG/ULEAC (SMP)

8 Write down the equations of these lines.
   (a) 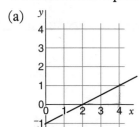   (b)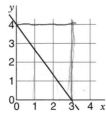

Answers and hints ► page 112

Solving linear equations

Equations with x on one side of the equation only

x is a number the value of which is unknown.

The **equation** $3x - 2 = 7$ means that the expression $3x - 2$ is equal to 7.

The value of x for which this is true is called the **solution** to the equation.
To **solve** (find the solution of) an equation we use the fact that an equation is still true if

- the same number is added to (or subtracted from) each side or
- each side is multiplied (or divided) by the same number

You may be able to guess that $x = 3$, but this is how you **solve** $3x - 2 = 7$:

$$3x - 2 = 7 \quad \boxed{\text{Add 2 to each side}} \Rightarrow 3x = 9 \quad \boxed{\text{Divide both sides by 3}} \Rightarrow x = 3$$

Check by substituting the value 3 for x in the left-hand side of the equation, that is $(3 \times 3) - 2 = 7$, which equals the right-hand side.

Here is one way to solve $\frac{x}{7} + 4 = 10$.

$$\frac{x}{7} + 4 = 10 \quad \boxed{\text{Subtract 4 from each side}} \Rightarrow \frac{x}{7} = 6 \quad \boxed{\text{Multiply both sides by 7}} \Rightarrow x = 42$$

Check by substituting the value 42 for x in the left-hand side of the equation, that is $\frac{42}{7} + 4 = 6 + 4 = 10$, which equals the right-hand side.

Remember that solutions are not always positive whole numbers.

Equations with x on both sides of the equation

Here is a way to solve an equation like $5x + 7 = 3x - 10$.

Subtract $3x$ from both sides.	$2x + 7 = {}^-10$
Subtract 7 from both sides.	$2x = {}^-17$
Divide both sides by 2.	$x = \frac{^-17}{2} = {}^-8\frac{1}{2}$

Check that you understand this working.

Check by substituting in both $5x + 7$ and $3x - 10$: $\quad {}^-42\frac{1}{2} + 7 = {}^-35\frac{1}{2}$ and ${}^-25\frac{1}{2} - 10 = {}^-35\frac{1}{2}$

---

1 Solve each of these equations.

(a) $2x - 2 = 8$ (b) $8a = 4$ (c) $^-9 = 3x$ (d) $2x - 10 = 0$

(e) $\frac{x}{3} = 4$ (f) $6 + \frac{x}{2} = 9$ (g) $2(x + 3) = 22$ (h) $\frac{x + 7}{3} = 2$

2 Use a calculator to help you solve these equations. Give your answers correct to 2 decimal places.

(a) $1 \cdot 7x + 15 \cdot 7 = 33 \cdot 4$ (b) $31 \cdot 2 - 4a = 1 \cdot 6$ (c) $\frac{x}{4 \cdot 3} = 7 \cdot 1$

3 Solve these equations.

(a) $3x - 5 = x - 10$ (b) $2(x + 10) = 25 + 4x$ (c) $\frac{1}{2}x - 3 = 5 + x$

(d) $2 - 3x = 14$ (e) $4p + 2 = p + 11$ (f) $\frac{1}{2}(2x - 1) = {}^-11$

(g) $3x + 7 = 5x + 1$ (h) $m - \frac{4m}{7} = 12$ (i) $\frac{1}{2}(x - 2) = 11 - x$

Answers and hints ► page 113

Brackets and factors

The expression $2(c + 8)$ can be written as $2c + 16$.
When we remove the brackets we multiply each term inside by 2.

Brackets
► page 23

Sometimes we need to reverse this process. In the expression $10x + 15y$,
5 divides into (is a factor of) both $10x$ and $15y$, so we can write

Factors
► page 2

$$10x + 15y = 5(2x + 3y).$$

This reverse process is called **factorising**.

Check that you understand this factorisation of $6a + 10ab$.
2 is a factor of both $6a$ and $10ab$ so we can write

$$6a + 10ab = 2(3a + 5ab).$$

But a is a factor of both $3a$ and $5ab$, so we can also write

$$6a + 10ab = 2a(3 + 5b).$$

◁ *This is the simplest form.*
*(There are no more **common factors**.)*

The rules of indices

You need to know how to simplify an algebraic expression involving indices.
The rules for any numbers x, a and b are

Indices
► page 18

$$x^a \times x^b = x^{a+b}, \quad x^a \div x^b = x^{a-b} \quad \text{and} \quad (x^a)^b = x^{ab}.$$

Check that you agree with these:

$$(2x)^2 = (2x) \times (2x) = 4x^2 \qquad 2x^2 \times 3x^5 = 6x^{(2+5)} = 6x^7 \qquad 6x^5 \div 3x^3 = 2x^{5-3} = 2x^2$$

Note that the only way to simplify, say, $4x^3 + x^2$, is to factorise it: $4x^3 + x^2 = x^2(4x + 1)$

1   Copy and complete these:
   (a) $2x + 8 = 2(x + ...)$ (b) $3a - 12b = 3(... - ...)$ (c) $4x + xy = x(... + ...)$
   (d) $4x + 20y = 4(..........)$ (e) $x^2 + 4x = x(... + ...)$ (f) $8ab - 12b = 4b(... - ...)$
   (g) $^-x^2 - 3x = ^-x(... + ...)$ (h) $^-5n^2 - 30n = ^-5n(... + ...)$ (i) $^-2x^2 + 4x = ^-2x(..........)$

2   Factorise these expressions.
   (a) $5a + 20b$ (b) $4a + ab$ (c) $n^2 + 3n$ (d) $2x + 6x^2$
   (e) $8xy + 12y$ (f) $4x^2 - 12x$ (g) $4mn - 8n^2$ (h) $^-x^2 + 2x$

3   Where possible simplify these expressions.
   (a) $(4a^2)^2$ (b) $(2a^3)^2$ (c) $2x^3 + 3x^2$ (d) $x \times 2x^2$
   (e) $5c^4 \div c$ (f) $3c^5 \div c^3$ (g) $3x^2 \times 2x^3$ (h) $3(2x^2)^3$

4   Write down three different algebraic expressions which are equivalent
   to each of these:
   (a) $24ab$ (b) $24a^2b$ (c) $25x^3$

Answers and hints ► page 114

Time graphs

Graphs that show how a quantity varies over a period of time
can be used to 'tell a story' about what was happening.

A man cycles up a hill, rests at the top and then
'freewheels' down the other side.
The graph shows the distance he cycled during these three stages of his journey.

He cycled up the hill at a constant **rate**.
The graph for this section is a sloping straight line.
It shows that he travelled 1200 m in 5 minutes
(which is $5 \times 60 = 300$ seconds).
So his speed was $1200 \div 300 = 4$ m/s.

The cyclist rested for 4 minutes.
This part of the graph is a straight
horizontal line – his speed is 0 m/s!

For the last part, down the
hill, he was getting faster
and faster, not cycling at a
constant speed.
The fact that the graph is
curved shows that his
speed was changing.

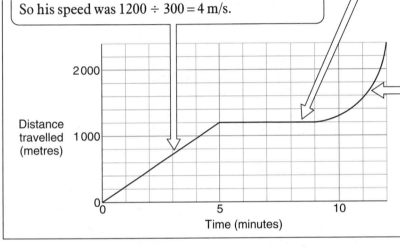

Distance travelled (metres)

Speed ► page 58

1   This graph shows the story of a girl
    trying to catch a bus.

    (a) What was her speed in metres
        per minute:
        (i) for the first 4 minutes
        (ii) between 4 and 5 minutes
        (iii) between 5 and 8 minutes
    (b) How far did she travel in the
        first 8 minutes?
    (c) Describe in words the story told
        by the graph.

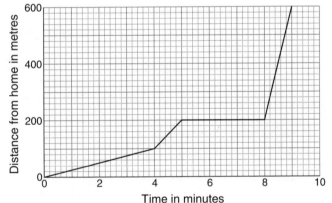

2   This sketch graph shows what happened
    to the volume of water in a bath.
    At the start the plug was put in and
    the hot tap was turned on full.

    (a) Describe what you think happened at A.

    (b) What happened at B?

    (c) What happened at C?

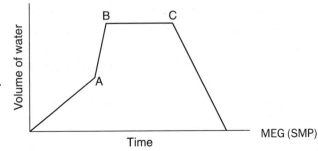

MEG (SMP)

28

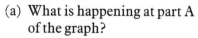

3 Delroy is driving his car along a straight road.
   This sketch graph shows how the speed
   of the car changes.

   (a) What is happening at part A
       of the graph?

   (b) What is happening at part B
       of the graph?

   (c) Look at the part of the graph from C to D.
       Describe what is happening on this part of the journey.

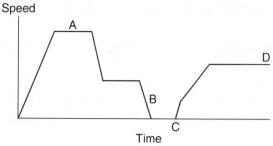

MEG (SMP)

4 Sketch a graph to show how the number of people changed
   at the concert described below.
   Use a grid like this:

   The Victoria Arena held 10000
   people. The arena was empty
   when the doors opened at 5 p.m.
   The number of people in the
   arena grew steadily.
   By about 7 p.m. it was half full.

   Then there was a rush of
   people. The arena filled very
   quickly. It was full at 8 p.m. The
   concert lasted until 11 p.m.
   The arena then emptied, slowly
   at first, then speeding up. It was
   empty by 12 p.m.

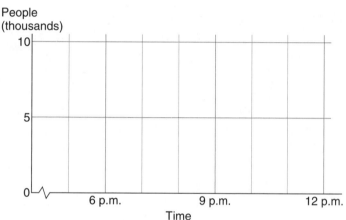

5 A train from King's Cross stops at Finsbury Park, Stevenage,
   Hitchin and Cambridge. The time the train takes to get to each station
   and its distance from King's Cross are shown in this table.

	Time from King's Cross (minutes)	Distance from King's Cross (km)
King's Cross	0	0
Finsbury Park	4	5
Stevenage	26	43
Hitchin	33	50
Cambridge	68	92

   (a) Show this journey on a time graph.
       Assume the train travels at a steady speed between each station.

   (b) Which is the fastest part of the journey?

   (c) What is the average speed of the train over this part?

Answers and hints ► page 114

Drawing and using non-linear graphs

You need to be able to draw graphs of equations such as

$$y = x^2 - 2x, \ y = x^3 \text{ and } y = \frac{5}{x}.$$

Drawing straight line graphs ► page 24

As the graphs are not straight lines you need several points to define the curve.

To draw the graph of $y = x^2 - 2x$ first complete a table of values by substituting in the equation.

Substitution ► page 23

x	$^-2$	$^-1$	0	1	2	3	4
y	8	3	0	$^-1$	0	3	8

Check that you agree with these values of y.

Then choose and draw suitable axes and plot the points. The graph on the right has been reduced but in an exam you would be given 2 mm graph paper with the axes labelled.

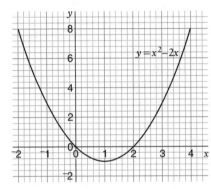

Recognising graphs ► page 38

Finally, draw as smooth a curve as possible through the points. (If you find a 'rogue' point, check it carefully. You will probably have made a mistake.)

To draw the graph of $y = \frac{5}{x}$, start with a table of values.

x	$^-5$	$^-4$	$^-2$	$^-1$	1	2	4	5
y	$^-1$	$^-1{\cdot}25$	$^-2{\cdot}5$	$^-5$	5	$2{\cdot}5$	$1{\cdot}25$	1

The graph is unusual because there is no value of y corresponding to $x = 0$.

(Another form of the equation $y = \frac{5}{x}$ is $xy = 5$.)

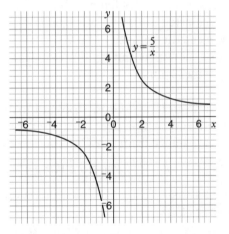

Algebraic relationships are sometimes referred to as **formulas**. They usually apply to real-life situations like those in questions 3 to 6.

You will need 2 mm graph paper for these questions.

1 (a) Copy and complete this table of values.

x	$^-2$	$^-1$	0	1	2	3	4	5
$x^2 - 3x$					$^-2$			10
$^-x^2 + 3x$	$^-10$		0			0		

(b) Draw a grid with x-values from $^-3$ to 5 and y-values from $^-10$ to 10.
On your grid draw and label the two curves $y = x^2 - 3x$ and $y = ^-x^2 + 3x$.
What do you notice?

2   For each of these questions copy and complete the table for the equation given.
    Then draw the graph using axes as descibed.

(a) $y = 3x^2 - 4x + 1$

x	⁻4	⁻3	⁻2	⁻1	0	1	2	3	4
y	65			8	1			16	

   x-values from ⁻4 to 4 (using a scale of 1 cm to 1 unit) and y-values from 0 to 70
   (using 1 cm to 10 units)

(b) $y = x^3$

x	⁻3	⁻2	⁻1	0	1	2	3
y		⁻8		0			

   x-values from ⁻3 to 3 (using 1 cm to 1 unit) and y-values from ⁻30 to 30 (using 1 cm to 10 units)

(c) $y = \dfrac{12}{x}$

x	⁻6	⁻4	⁻3	⁻2	⁻1	1	2	3	4	6
y			⁻4		⁻12	12				2

   x-values from ⁻6 to 6 (using 1 cm to 1 unit) and y-values from ⁻12 to 12 (using 1 cm to 2 units)

3   A firm makes a range of cylindrical water tanks.
    Each tank has the same height.

    The volume, V m³, of a tank with radius x metres
    is given by the formula

$$V = 6x^2.$$

    The table shows the values of V for the given values of x.

x	0	1	2	3	4
V	0	6	24	54	96

(a) Draw axes with x-values from 0 to 4 (using 2 cm to 1 unit)
    and V-values from 0 to 100 (using 1 cm to 10 units).
    Plot points to represent these values.
    Join up your points with a smooth curve.

(b) Use your graph to estimate
     (i) the volume of a tank with a radius of 2·5 m,
    (ii) the radius of a tank with a volume of 20 m³.

MEG (SMP)

4   The volume of gas, V, in a sealed container decreases as the pressure, P, increases.
    The formula connecting V and P is $V = \dfrac{10}{P}$.

(a) Calculate the two missing volumes in this table.

P (N/cm²)	1	2	4	5	8	10
V (cm³)		5		2	1·25	1

(b) Draw a horizontal P-axis from 0 to 10 with a scale of 1 cm to 1 N/cm²
    and a vertical V-axis from 0 to 12 with a scale of 1 cm to 1 cm³.
    Draw the graph of $V = \dfrac{10}{P}$.

(c) Estimate the value of V when $P = 3$ from your graph.

(d) Does V ever become zero? Explain your answer.

5 A stone is catapulted vertically upwards at a speed of 30 m/s.
The height, h metres, of the stone above the ground after t seconds
is given by the formula

$$h = 30t - 5t^2.$$

(a) Use the formula to find the missing value in this table.

t (seconds)	0	1	2	3	4	5	6
h (metres)	0	25	40		40	25	0

(b) Draw a horizontal t-axis from 0 to 6 (with a scale of 2 cm to 1 second) and
a vertical h-axis from 0 to 50 (with a scale of 1 cm to 5 metres).
Plot the points from the table onto your grid.
Join up the points with a smooth curve.

(c) Use your graph to find when the stone is 30 metres above the ground. MEG (SMP)

6 When a driver tries to stop a car quickly the car may skid.
The length of the skid depends on the speed of the car.
This formula tells you roughly the length of the skid.

$l = \dfrac{s^2}{200}$ l is the length of the skid in metres.
s is the speed of the car in kilometres per hour.

(a) Calculate the two missing skid lengths (in metres) in this table.

s	20	40	60	80	100	120
l	2	8	18			72

(b) Draw a horizontal s-axis from 0 to 130 (with a scale of 1 cm to 10 km per hour)
and a vertical l-axis from 0 to 100 (with a scale of 1 cm to 10 metres).
Plot the values in the table and draw a smooth curve through the points.

Use your graph to answer parts (c) and (d).

(c) Estimate the length of a skid when the car is travelling at
90 kilometres per hour.

(d) The length of a skid is 24 metres. Estimate the speed of the car. MEG (SMP)

Answers and hints ▶ page 115

Changing the subject of a formula

A **formula** shows the relationship between quantities.
The formula for the volume V of a pyramid of height h and base area A is $V = \frac{1}{3}Ah$.
We say that V is the **subject** of the formula.

It is possible to make A the subject of the formula (to make $A = ...$).
Remember that an equation remains true if you do the same to both sides.
Check that you can follow this working.

Solving linear
equations ► page 26

$$V = \tfrac{1}{3}Ah$$

$$3V = Ah \qquad \text{Both sides of the equation multiplied by 3.}$$

$$\frac{3V}{h} = A \qquad \text{Both sides divided by } h.$$

So $\quad A = \dfrac{3V}{h}$ ◁ (This is a formula for A in terms of V and h.)

The formula $v = u + ft$ is used in physics.
Convince yourself that these changes of subject are correct.

$$v = u + ft$$
$$v - ft = u \qquad (ft \text{ subtracted})$$
So $\qquad u = v - ft$

$$v = u + ft$$
$$v - u = ft \qquad (u \text{ subtracted})$$
$$t = \frac{v - u}{f} \qquad (\text{divided by} f)$$

---

1 Rearrange each of these formulas to make the letter in square brackets the new subject.

(a) $e = w + 5$ $[w]$ (b) $b = a - 3$ $[a]$ (c) $C = \pi d$ $[d]$ (d) $l = 2e + 5$ $[e]$

(e) $y = mx + c$ $[x]$ (f) $A = \dfrac{h(a + b)}{2}$ $[h]$ (g) $R = \dfrac{V}{I}$ $[I]$ (h) $s = \dfrac{t(u + v)}{2}$ $[v]$

2 The formula for the total length of edges, L, for this box is $L = 4(2a + b)$.
Rearrange this formula to make b the subject.

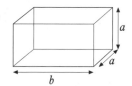

3 A formula used by electricians is $V = \dfrac{W}{A}$.

Make A the subject of this formula.

MEG (SMP)

4 The cost, C pence, of printing n party invitations is given by $C = 120 + 40n$.
Find a formula for n in terms of C.

MEG

5 The formula for finding the
volume ($V\,\text{cm}^3$) of this prism is
$$V = \frac{bhl}{2}$$

where b, h and l are measured in centimetres.

(a) Rearrange the formula to make h the subject.

(b) Calculate h when $b = 2{\cdot}5$, $l = 8$ and $V = 24$.

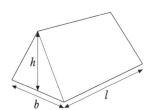

Answers and hints ► page 117

Inequalities and regions

Algebraic statements usually involve one of the following symbols:

$=$	is equal to	$\neq$	is not equal to
$>$	is greater than	$<$	is less than
$\geq$	is greater than or equal to	$\leq$	is less than or equal to

A statement involving $>, \geq, <$ or $\leq$ is called an **inequality**.

Equations remain true if 'you do the same to both sides', but we need to find if the same is true for inequalities.

Solving linear equations ► page 26

Suppose we start with an inequality, say, $3 < 5$.

- It remains true if we add, subtract, multiply by or divide by a positive number.
- It also remains true if we add or subtract a negative number.
- However, if we **multiply or divide by a negative number, the direction of the inequality reverses.**

> Check these three statements by using, say, 5 and ⁻5.

Check that you can follow the solutions of these inequalities.

$$x > 8 + 2x$$

Subtract $2x$ from both sides. $^-x > 8$
Multiply both sides by $^-1$, $x < ^-8$
remembering to reverse the sign.

> Check by substituting, say, $x = ^-9$ into both sides of the original inequality.

$$^-3x < 12 - x$$

Add x to both sides. $^-2x < 12$
Divide both sides by $^-2$, $x > ^-6$
remembering to reverse the sign.

> Check by substituting, say, $x = ^-5$ into both sides of the original inequality.

The inequality $x > ^-6$ can be shown on a graph. The line $x = ^-6$ is the boundary between the two **regions** $x > ^-6$ and $x < ^-6$.

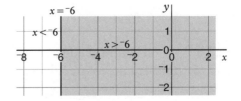

Suppose you wanted to show the region $y > 2x + 3$ on a graph.

- Start by drawing the line $y = 2x + 3$.
- Test points on both sides of the line to find the region where $y > 2x + 3$.
- Shade the region.

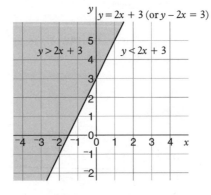

Drawing straight line graphs ► page 24

1   Solve these inequalities.
    Check your solutions by substituting some suitable numbers
    into the original inequality.

   (a) $x + 5 > 8$ (b) $x - 3 \geq 4$ (c) $^{-}2a < 4$ (d) $2b + 5 < b + 20$

   (e) $a - 1 \geq 2a - 4$ (f) $^{-}10 < 2c$ (g) $\frac{x}{2} \leq 3$ (h) $5(x + 1) > 2(x + 7)$

2   Find all the whole number solutions to   (a) $^{-}3 < a \leq 2$ (b) $^{-}4 \leq 2a < 8$.

3   $6 \leq n < 16$
    Write down the even whole numbers which satisfy this inequality.   MEG/ULEAC (SMP)

4   Ajaz said 'I thought of a whole number, multiplied it by 3 then subtracted 2.
    The answer was between 47 and 62'.
    List the whole numbers that Ajaz could have used.   MEG

5   The sum of three consecutive whole numbers $n, n + 1$ and $n + 2$ is less than 48.

   (a) Write this as an inequality and solve it.

   (b) What are the largest possible three numbers that sum to less than 48?

6   The length of each side of a triangle is less
    than the sum of the other two sides.
    Use this information to write down
    three inequalities for this triangle.
    Solve each of the inequalities.

   (All lengths are in centimetres.)

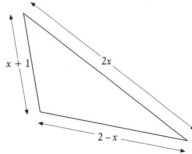

7   Solve the inequality $1 \leq 2 - x < 4$, where x is a whole number.

8   Write down the inequality which describes each of these shaded regions.
    Check your answers by using some test points.

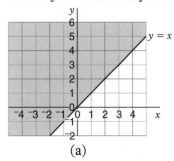
(a)

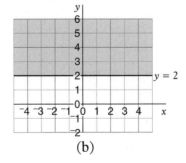
(b)

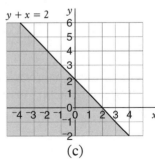
(c)

9   On squared paper draw four grids with values of x and y from $^{-}6$ to 6.
    Shade and label each of these regions on a separate grid.

   (a) $y > 2x$ (b) $y < x + 1$ (c) $y > 2x - 3$ (d) $2y + x < 4$

Answers and hints ▶ page 117

Simultaneous equations

Graphical solution

Look at the lines drawn on the grid.

There is only one point that fits both equations.

This is the point $(2, 3)$ where the two lines cross.

We say that $x = 2$ and $y = 3$ are the solutions to the pair of **simultaneous equations** $2y + x = 8$ and $y + 1 = 2x$.

Always check your solutions by substituting them back into the original equations.

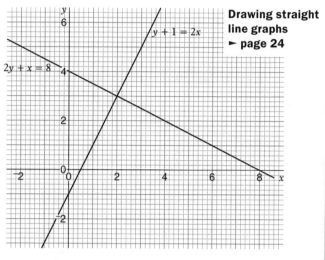

Drawing straight line graphs
► **page 24**

You need 2 mm graph paper for questions 1 to 5.

1 (a) Draw the graphs of the equations
  (i) $y = 2x + 1$
  (ii) $2y + 3x = 6$
  (Use a grid with values of x and y from $^-2$ to 3 and a scale of 2 cm to 1 unit.)

  (b) Use your graphs to solve the simultaneous equations
$$y = 2x + 1$$
$$2y + 3x = 6$$

MEG (SMP)

2 Draw two grids with values of x and y from $^-2$ to 8 and a scale of 1 cm to 1 unit.
Use a graphical method to solve each of the two pairs of simultaneous equations.
Give your answers correct to 1 decimal place.

  (a) $7x + 4y = 28$ and $4x + 5y = 20$
  (b) $2y - x = 3$ and $3y + 2x = 9$

3 Draw a grid with values of x and y from $^-2$ to 6 and a scale of 1 cm to 1 unit.
Draw graphs to solve, correct to 1 decimal place, the simultaneous equations
$$4y + 5x = 20 \quad \text{and} \quad 2x - y = 0$$

MEG

4 Use a graphical method to find which values of a and b fit both these equations.
$$2a + b = 4, \qquad 3a = 1 + b$$

5 Solve the equations $y - x = 1$ and $8 = 2y + x$ graphically.

Finding a solution without using a graph

Here are two methods of solving algebraically
the simultaneous equations

$2y + x = 8$ and $y + 1 = 2x$.

Solving linear equations
► page 26

Method 1

Write out the two equations and label them.

$$2y + x = 8 \quad \text{(equation A)}$$
$$y + 1 = 2x \quad \text{(equation B)}$$

If necessary rewrite one equation so that it is
in the same form as the other.

$$y - 2x = {}^-1 \quad \text{(equation B rewritten)}$$

If necessary multiply one equation to give a
pair of equal terms in either x or y.

$$\Updownarrow$$
$$4y + 2x = 16 \quad \text{(equation A multiplied by 2)}$$

Add or subtract both sides of the equations
that you now have, to remove the equal terms.

$$5y = 15 \quad \text{(the two equations added together)}$$
$$\text{So } y = 3$$

Substitute in equation A or B to find x or y. $(2 \times 3) + x = 8$ ($y = 3$ substituted into equation A)

$$\text{So } x = 2$$

Always check your results by substituting them back in the 'other' equation:

   Left-hand side of equation B $= 3 + 1 = 4$;   right-hand side $= 2 \times 2 = 4$

Method 2

Here you substitute at the start.
You need to be especially careful with the algebra.

From equation B we know that $y = 2x - 1$.
Substituting this expression for y in equation A gives

$$2(2x - 1) + x = 8$$
$$4x - 2 + x = 8$$
$$5x - 2 = 8$$
$$5x = 10$$
$$x = 2$$

Substitute $x = 2$ in equation B, say, to find the value of y. $y = (2 \times 2) - 1 = 3$

Check in A: left-hand side $= (2 \times 3) + 2 = 8$, which is the right-hand side.

---

6   Solve each of these pairs of simultaneous equations by the method of your choice.
   Check your answers.

   (a) $x + 3y = 10$, $x + y = 4$ (b) $2x + 3y = 13$, $x + 2y = 8$

   (c) $x + y = {}^-1$, $2x - y = 4$ (d) $x + 2y = 10$, $3x + y = 0$

   (e) $x - 2y = 4$, $3x + 2y = 8$ (f) $2x + y = 4$, $x - 3y = 9$

   (g) $4y = x + 8$, $4y + x = 4$ (h) $3a + 4b = 10$, $a = 3 - b$

7   Without drawing a graph, find the coordinates of the point where
   these two lines meet.

   $$5x + 2y = 16 \quad \text{and} \quad 3x - y = 3$$

Answers and hints ► page 118

Recognising graphs

These have the same shape as $y = ax^2$,
but they cut the y-axis in a different place.

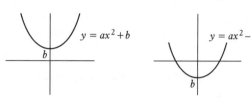

You need to be able to recognise these graphs
and sketch them from memory.

a is **positive**.

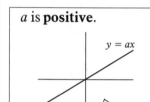 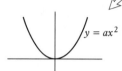 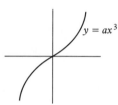 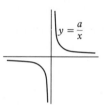

a is **negative**.

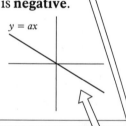 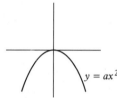 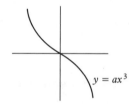 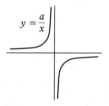

A straight line through $(0, 0)$ shows that y is proportional to x.
In the equation $y = ax$, the value a is the **gradient**.
If the graph is about a practical situation,
the gradient often tells you the **rate** at which something changes.

Proportion ► page 14
Gradient ► pages 24, 62
Rates ► pages 28, 58
Drawing non-linear graphs
► page 30

1 (a) By drawing a graph or otherwise, find in which of these tables y is proportional to x.

(i)

x	15	20	25	35
y	10	20	30	50

(ii)

x	10	25	35	40
y	12	30	42	48

(iii)

x	0	10	30	40
y	20	25	35	40

(b) Where y is proportional to x, write down an equation connecting y and x in the form $y = ...$

2 This graph shows the volume of water
in a bath as it is being filled.

(a) At what rate is the bath filling?

(b) V is the volume of water in the bath
in litres and t is the time in minutes
since the tap was turned on.
Write down a formula connecting V and t.

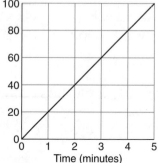

MEG (SMP)

3   Boxes are pushed along a horizontal table.
    The force, F, needed to move each box is proportional to
    the mass m of the box.

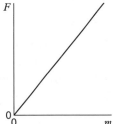

(a) What are the missing values in the table?

Mass m (kg)	1·5	0·5	
Force F (newtons)	4·5		5·4

(b) This is a sketch of the graph of the results.
    (i) What is the gradient of the graph?
    (ii) Write down the equation connecting F and m in the form
        $F = \dots m$.

4   A student studying electricity varied the voltage across a piece of wire
    and measured the current in the wire each time. Here are her results.

Voltage (V)	0	3·0	4·2	6·4	8·6	10·0
Current (I)	0	4·2	7·2	9·4	12·8	14·8

(a) Plot these on a graph with a vertical I-axis from 0 to 15
    and a horizontal V-axis from 0 to 10.

(b) Draw a line of best fit through the six points.
    (The current is directly proportional to the voltage.)

(c) Find the gradient of the graph.

(d) Write down the equation connecting I and V in the form $I = \dots V$.

5   Which of these equations goes with each graph? $y=3x^3$ $y=3x+4$ $y = 4x^2 + 3$ $y = \dfrac{4}{x}$

(a) 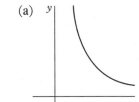   (b) 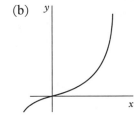   (c) 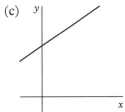   (d)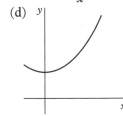

6   Below each graph is a list of equations.
    From each list select the one which could be the equation of the graph above.

(a) 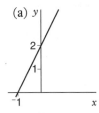   (b) 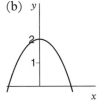   (c) 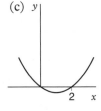   (d) 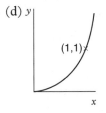   (e)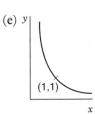

(a)
(i) $y = 2x - 2$
(ii) $y = 2x + 2$
(iii) $y = x + 2$

(b)
(i) $y = {}^-x^2 + 2$
(ii) $y = x^2 - 2$
(iii) $y = x^2 - 2x$

(c)
(i) $y = x^2 + 2x$
(ii) $y = x^2 + 2$
(iii) $y = x^2 - 2x$

(d)
(i) $y = x^2 + x$
(ii) $y = x^3$
(iii) $y = x^3 + x$

(e)
(i) $y = x^2$
(ii) $y = \dfrac{1}{x}$
(iii) $y = 2x^2 - 1$

Answers and hints ▶ page 119

Trial and improvement; graphical solution

You need to be able to solve cubic equations like $x^3 - 5x = 2$.
Here are two methods you can use for solving cubic, and other, equations.

Using trial and improvement

In this method we try different values of x until one is found
that gives $x^3 - 5x$ a value of 2.
Follow the working in the table, which starts with $x = 2$
as a reasonable first trial value.

> You need to make this as close as possible to 2.

Substitution ► page 23

Significant figures ► page 6

Trial value of x	Value of $x^3 - 5x$
2	⁻2
3	12
2·5	3·125
2·2	⁻0·352
2·4	1·824
2·45	2·456

> $x = 2$ is too small and $x = 3$ is too large, so the solution is between 2 and 3.

> The solution is between 2·2 and 2·5.

> The solution is between 2·4 and 2·45. So the solution to 2 s.f. is 2·4.

Check that the solution correct to 3 s.f. is 2·41.

If you are careful this should not take more than about six trials.

Using graphs

An alternative method for solving $x^3 - 5x = 2$
is to use graph paper or a graphical calculator.

- Plot the graphs $y = x^3 - 5x$ and $y = 2$
  on the same grid.

- Find the x-values of the points where
  the two graphs intersect. These are
  the solutions to the equation $x^3 - 5x = 2$.

As you can see, the equation has three solutions.

> This is the solution found by trial and improvement above.

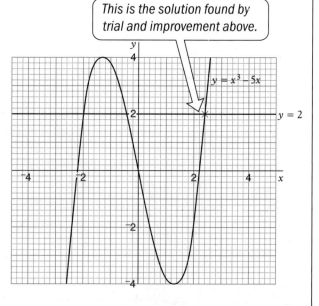

Drawing graphs ► pages 24, 30

1   Use trial and improvement to find, correct to 2 significant figures,
the solution between 0 and 10 to the equation $x^3 - 2x^2 = 2$.
Show your trials.

2   (a) Find the value of $x^3 + 5x$ when $x = 3.7$.

(b) Use trial and improvement to find a solution to $x^3 + 5x = 60$.
Give the value of x correct to 1 decimal place.   MEG/ULEAC (SMP)

3   Use trial and improvement to solve the equation $x^3 = 40$.
Write down all your trials.
Find the solution correct to 2 decimal places.   MEG (SMP)

You need 2 mm graph paper for questions 4 to 6.

4   (a) Copy and complete this table for $y = x^2$.

x	$^-3$	$^-2$	$^-1$	0	1	2	3
y							

(b) Draw the graph $y = x^2$. Use x-values from $^-3$ to 3 (2 cm to 1 unit)
and y-values from $^-1$ to 9 (1 cm to 1 unit).

(c) On the same axes, draw the graph of $y = 3 - x$, choosing values of
x between $^-3$ and 3.

(d) Solve the equation $x^2 = 3 - x$ by finding the values of x where the
two graphs cross.   MEG/ULEAC (SMP)

5   (a) Copy and complete the following table of values for $y = \dfrac{8}{x}$.

x	$^-8$	$^-7$	$^-6$	$^-5$	$^-4$	$^-3$	$^-2$	$^-1$	1	2	3	4	5	6	7	8
y		$^-1.1$	$^-1.3$	$^-1.6$	$^-2$		$^-2.7$	$^-4$	$^-8$			2.7				

(b) Using a scale of 1 cm to represent 1 unit on both the x-axis and the y-axis,
draw the graph of $y = \dfrac{8}{x}$ for values of x from $^-8$ to $^-1$ and from 1 to 8.

(c) Draw the line $y = x - 1$ on the same axes.

(d) Use your graphs to find the two solutions of the equation $x - 1 = \dfrac{8}{x}$.   MEG

6   (a) Given that $y = x^2 - 2x$, copy and complete the following table.

x	$^-1$	$^-0.5$	0	1	2	2.5	3
y		1.25	0	$^-1$	0		

(b) Using a scale of 4 cm to represent 1 unit on each axis,
draw the graph of $y = x^2 - 2x$ for values of x from $^-1$ to 3.

(c) Use your graph to find two solutions to the equation $x^2 - 2x = 1.5$.   MEG

Answers and hints ► page 120

Setting up expressions and equations

Rose is thinking of a number.
If she multiplies it by 4 and subtracts 9 she gets the same as
half the number plus 12.
What number is Rose thinking of?

Let the number be x.

Multiply it by 4	$4x$
Subtract 9	$4x - 9$

Halve the original number	$\frac{1}{2}x$
Add 12	$\frac{1}{2}x + 12$

To find Rose's number, solve the equation $\quad 4x - 9 = \frac{1}{2}x + 12.$

Solving linear equations ► page 26

Multiply both sides by 2 to remove the fraction. $\quad 8x - 18 = x + 24$

Rearrange the equation. $\qquad\qquad\qquad 7x = 42$

$$x = 6$$

So Rose must be thinking of the number 6.

Check by substituting back in the **original explanation**.
Do not use your expressions in case they are wrong.

1   The sum of the numbers on any two opposite faces of a normal dice is 7.

    (a) The number showing on the top of the dice is x.
        What is the number showing on the bottom?

    (b) The sum of two top numbers is y.
        What is the sum of the two bottom numbers?

2   Write down an algebraic expression for this.
    'Subtract 2 from a and multiply the result by 3.'

3   Scott is thinking of a number.
    Four times his number minus seven is equal to three times the number plus eight.
    Write this as an equation and solve it to find the number Scott is thinking of.

4   The middle number of three consecutive whole numbers is n.

    (a) What are the three consecutive numbers?

    (b) What is their sum?

5   Two angles in a triangle are $a°$ and $b°$. Write an expression for the third angle.

6   A certain number is multiplied by 7, and 13 is added to the result.
    The final number is 69.

    (a) Set up an equation to find the original number.

    (b) What was the original number?

7   One flock of sheep has 20 less than twice the number in a second flock.
    Together both flocks have 244 sheep. How many are there in each flock?

8 A theatre has 420 seats. Tickets for a play normally cost £8 each,
but advance bookings can be made for £5.
On a night when the theatre is full, the total takings are £2460.
Let x be the number of advance bookings made.

(a) Write down, in terms of x, the number of tickets not booked in advance.

(b) Write down an equation satisfied by x.

(c) Solve this equation to find the number of advance bookings made.   WJEC

9 Find the length and width
of this rectangle.
It has a perimeter of 24 units.

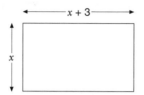

10 A school trip uses 36-seater buses and 12-seater minibuses.
The hire cost of a bus is £100 and the hire cost of a minibus is £80.

(a) Write down expressions for:
 (i) the number of passengers that can be carried by x buses and y minibuses.
 (ii) the hire cost in pounds of x buses and y minibuses.

(b) If 240 passengers have to be carried and the total cost of hire
must not be greater than £1000, write down two inequalities
that must be satisfied by x and y.

11 Write these statements as 'algebraic sentences'.

(a) 5 kg of potatoes at x pence per kilogram cost more than 90 pence.

(b) The perimeter of a triangle with sides a cm, b cm and c cm
is at least 60 cm.

(c) The area of a rectangle of length 10 cm and width x cm
cannot be more than 100 cm².

12 This drawing shows the total height for each stack of chairs.

(a) What is the total height of 6 chairs?

(b) If h cm is the height of the stack and c is the number of chairs in a stack,
write a formula for h in terms of c.

(c) What is the greatest number of chairs stacked in this way
which could be slid through a doorway 196 cm high?   MEG/ULEAC (SMP)

Quadratics

Expanding double brackets

Make sure you can multiply out single brackets and can use the reverse process to factorise expressions using one bracket.

Removing brackets ► page 23
Brackets and factors ► page 27

You also need to know how to multiply out (expand) double brackets, for example $(x + 2)(x + 5)$.

A multiplication grid is very useful for multiplying out an expression like this. It means there is less risk of missing out terms.

$$(x + 2)(x + 5)$$

×	x	5
x	x^2	$5x$
2	$2x$	10

$$\text{Total} = x^2 + 5x + 2x + 10$$
$$= x^2 + 7x + 10$$
$$\text{so } (x + 2)(x + 5) = x^2 + 7x + 10$$

Solving quadratic equations by factors

Equations like $x^2 + 5x - 6 = 0$, $z^2 + 3z = 0$ and $x^2 + 6 = 5x$ are called **quadratic equations**.
They usually have two different solutions.

Convince yourself, by substituting, that $z = 0$ and $z = {}^-3$ are both solutions of $z^2 + 3z = 0$.

One way to solve a quadratic equation is by factorising.

Solving equations by trial and improvement ► page 40
Solving equations by plotting a graph ► page 40

Example
Solve $4x^2 - 12x = 0$.

If we factorise $4x^2 - 12x = 0$
we get $4x(x - 3) = 0$.

If the product of two numbers is zero, then one or both of them must be zero.

So either $4x = 0$ or $x - 3 = 0$
This means that $x = 0$ and $x = 3$ are both solutions of $4x^2 - 12x = 0$.
(Check by substituting these values back in the equation.)

Example
Solve $x^2 + 5x - 6 = 0$ by factorisation.

Start by factorising the expression $x^2 + 5x - 6$.

$$x^2 + 5x - 6 = (x - 1)(x + 6)$$

If $x^2 + 5x - 6 = 0$ then either $x - 1 = 0$ or $x + 6 = 0$.

So the solutions are $x = 1$ and $x = {}^-6$.
(Check by substituting back.)

You might find a multiplication grid helpful:

×	x	⁻1
x	x^2	^-x
6	$6x$	$^-6$

1 Multiply out these brackets and simplify each expression.

(a) $(x + 1)(x + 2)$ (b) $(x + 4)(x - 5)$ (c) $(x - 4)(x - 5)$

(d) $(a + 2)(a - 2)$ (e) $(2x + 1)(x + 4)$ (f) $(3x + 2)(2x - 3)$

(g) $(4x - 3)(3x - 5)$ (h) $(5a - 1)(6a + 8)$

2 Multiply out each of these expressions.

(a) $(x + 2)^2$ (b) $(x - 2)^2$ (c) $(2x + 1)^2$ (d) $(a + b)^2$

3 Copy and complete these factorisations.

(a) $x^2 + 7x + 12 = (x + 3)(x + ...)$ (b) $x^2 + 10x + 21 = (x + 3)(x + ...)$

(c) $x^2 + 2x - 15 = (x - ...)(x + 5)$ (d) $x^2 + 9x + 20 = (x + 4)(... + ...)$

(e) $x^2 - 6x + 8 = (x - ...)(x - ...)$ (f) $x^2 + 6x - 7 = (x - ....)(... ... ...)$

4 Find the values of x which fit these equations.

(a) $x(x - 3) = 0$ (b) $(x - 2)(x + 7) = 0$ (c) $(x + 2)(x - 9) = 0$

5 Solve these quadratic equations by factorising.

(a) $x^2 + 2x = 0$ (b) $2x^2 + x = 0$ (c) $x^2 - x - 20 = 0$

(d) $x^2 - 6x + 8 = 0$ (e) $x^2 + 3x - 10 = 0$ (f) $x^2 + 10x + 24 = 0$

(g) $x^2 + 4x - 5 = 0$ (h) $x^2 + x - 20 = 0$ (i) $x^2 - 10x + 21 = 0$

(j) $x^2 + 10 = {}^-7x$ (k) $x^2 - x = 12$ (l) $x^2 - 1 = 12x + 12$

Check your answers by substituting back into the original equations.

6 The diagram shows the plan of an L-shaped room of area $24\,\text{m}^2$.
All the lengths are in metres.

(a) Write the area of the floor in terms of x.

(b) Form a quadratic equation and solve it to find the value of x.

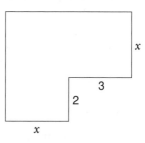

7 The diagram shows a rectangular patio made
from 1-metre paving slabs.

(a) Write down an expression for the area of
the patio in terms of x.

(b) If the area of the patio is 40 square metres,
find the value of x.

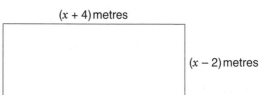

Answers and hints ► page 122

Sequences and terms

Look at this sequence: 2 6 10 14 ...
It goes up in fours.   The 1st term is 2.
                       The 2nd term is 6.
                       The 3rd term is 10.
                       The 4th term is 14.

> '...' is shorthand for 'and so on in the same way'.

Convince yourself that the nth term is $4n - 2$.

If you know the expression for the nth term it is easy to calculate, say, the 100th term: $(4 \times 100) - 2 = 398$.

> This is more efficient than adding on four 99 times to find the 100th term.

With some sequences you may need to experiment in order to find the correct expression for the nth term.
The expression must hold for all the terms which you know.

When looking for patterns in numbers it can be very useful to be able to recognise square and cube numbers.

Square and cube numbers
► page 2

1   Write down the first six terms of the sequence whose nth term is $3n + 2$.

2   For each number sequence write down the 6th term and the nth term.
   (a) 2 4 6 8 10 ...   (b) 4 5 6 7 8 ...   (c) 8 10 12 14 16 ...
   (d) 1 3 5 7 9 ...   (e) 1 4 9 16 25 ... (f) 2 5 10 17 26 ...

3   A pattern of tiles uses unshaded and shaded tiles like this:

   1st pattern 2nd pattern 3rd pattern

 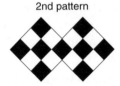

   (a) Draw the next pattern of tiles on a piece of square paper.

   (b) Copy and complete this table for this pattern of tiles.

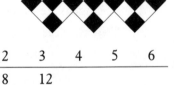

Pattern	1	2	3	4	5	6
Unshaded	4	8	12			
Shaded	5	9	13			

   (c) Write down an expression, in terms of n, for the number of shaded tiles in the nth pattern.

MEG (SMP)

4   Look at this sequence: 2   8   18   32
   (a) Write down the next three terms of the sequence.
   (b) Write down the nth term of the sequence.

MEG/ULEAC (SMP)

5   Here is a pattern of tiles made from numbers of white tiles (w) and grey tiles (g).
   Find a connection between w and g in the form $w = ...$

  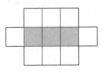

Answers and hints ► page 123

Mixed algebra

1   A printing firm prints leaflets at a standing charge of £20 plus
    £4 per pack of a hundred leaflets.

   (a) Write down the inequality for the number of packs of leaflets, n,
    which can be printed for £50 or less.

   (b) What is the largest number of packs that can be printed?

2   (a) Jane has a part-time job. This is how she works out her spending money:

      'My spending money is the number of hours worked times four,
    minus five for savings.'

      Write a formula for her spending money (P) in terms of the hours worked (H).

   (b) Solve the equations   (i) $3x - 5 = 7 - x$ (ii) $\frac{1}{2}x + 2 = 1$ MEG/ULEAC (SMP)

3   Use trial and improvement to find one solution of the equation $x^3 = 15$.
    Give your answer to two decimal places. Show all your trials.   MEG/ULEAC (SMP)

4   (a) Copy and complete the table below for $y = x^2 + 3$.

x	0	1	2	3	4	5	6
y		4		12			

   (b) Plot these points and hence draw the graph of $y = x^2 + 3$.
    (Use 2 cm for 1 unit on the x-axis and 2 cm for 5 units on the y-axis.)

   (c) Use your graph to solve the equation $x^2 + 3 = 30$.

5   (a) Look at this sequence: 1   2   5   14   ...

      'To find the next term multiply the last term by three and subtract one.'
    Use this rule to find the next two terms of the sequence.

   (b) Here is a sequence with a different rule: 1   2   4   7   11   ...

     (i) Write down the next two terms of this sequence.

     (ii) Explain how to get the 12th term from the 11th term.   MEG/ULEAC (SMP)

6   In the tennis championships at Wimbledon the players are given
    a set of new balls at the start of their match.
    They are given another set of new balls after they have played 7 games.
    After this they are given new balls after every 9 games.

   (a) Copy and complete this table.

Number of ball changes (x)	1	2	3	4	5
Number of games played (y)	7	16	25		

   (b) Write down the general rule connecting y and x in the form
    $y =$ some expression in x.

   (c) Rewrite your formula in (b) so that x is the subject.

Answers and hints ► page 124

SHAPE, SPACE AND MEASURES
Understanding shape

Reflection symmetry

Flat shapes may have **lines of symmetry**. If you put a mirror on a line of symmetry the shape will look the same.

Solid shapes may have **planes of symmetry**. If you chop the solid in half down a plane of symmetry and put half on a mirror, it will look the same.

Rotation symmetry

Flat shapes may have a **centre of symmetry**. If you turn a flat shape about a centre of symmetry it will fit on to itself. The number of different positions it will fit is called the **order of rotation**, or **order of rotation symmetry**. This shape has rotation symmetry of order 2.

Solid shapes may have an **axis of symmetry**. If you turn a solid shape about an **axis of symmetry**, it will fit onto itself. The number of different positions it will fit is called the **order of rotation**. This solid has order of rotation symmetry 4 about this axis.

Constructing triangles

Suppose you need to draw a triangle with sides 3·2 cm, 5·5 cm and 4·8 cm.

Draw any side first.

Set your compasses to 3·2 cm. Draw this arc.

Draw this arc, radius 4·8 cm. Join up the triangle.

Suppose you need to draw a triangle with side AB = 4·6 cm, AC = 3·5 cm and angle C = 120°.

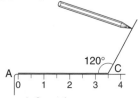

Draw AC and an angle of 120° at C.

Set your compasses to 4·6 cm and draw this arc, centre A.

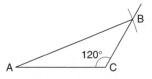

Join A to where the arc cuts the line from C.

Congruence

One shape is **congruent** to another when they have exactly the same shape and size. Here shape A is congruent to shape D.

1   (a) How many planes of symmetry does each of these objects have?

(i) 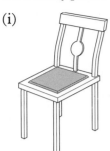   (ii)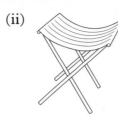

(b) Here are two shapes made from cubes.
Each of the shapes has rotation symmetry about the axis shown.
What is the order of rotation symmetry of each shape about the axis?   MEG (SMP)

(i) 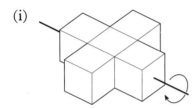   (ii)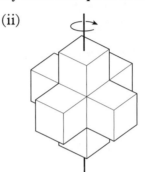

2   A design for a badge consists of
three congruent isosceles triangles
AEF, BFD, CDE placed within a
circle as shown.
AE = AF = 6·2 cm and EF = 4 cm.

(a) Use instruments to make a
full-size drawing of this design.

(b) Taking a measurement from your
drawing, write down the radius
of the circle passing through
A, B and C.

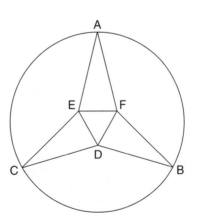

NICCEA

3   (a) Draw a triangle in which AB = 10 cm, BC = 8 cm and AC = 6 cm.

(b) Measure angle C.

4   Draw a triangle ABC in which AB = 7·5 cm, AC = 9 cm and angle B = 100°.

5   The lengths of the sides of a parallelogram are 2·5 cm and 4·7 cm.
One of the diagonals measures 3·6 cm.

(a) Draw the parallelogram.

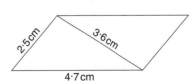

6 (a) Sketch each of the shapes below and draw all the lines of symmetry.

  (i) Square (ii) Equilateral triangle

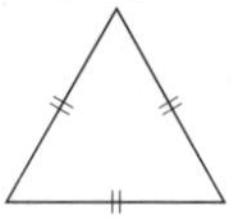

(b) Write down the order of rotational symmetry of

  (i) the square (ii) the equilateral triangle

ULEAC

7 In this ornamental window, state the shapes which are

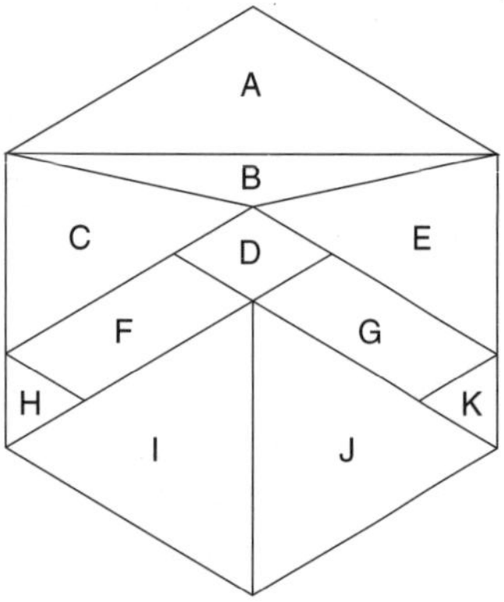

(a) equilateral triangles

(b) isosceles triangles

(c) parallelograms

(d) rhombuses

(e) similar to J, but not congruent to J

(f) congruent to C

Similarity ► page 62

MEG/ULEAC (SMP)

8 Five squares can be arranged in many different ways.
For example they could be made into a rectangle 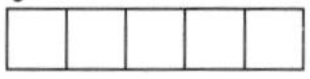
which has 2 lines of symmetry or
into this shape 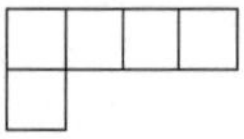 which has no lines of symmetry.

On squared paper show how 5 squares can be arranged into a shape which has

(a) 1 line of symmetry (b) 4 lines of symmetry (c) order of rotation symmetry 2

9 Copy and complete this table.
The names of the quadrilaterals may be chosen from the following list:
square, parallelogram, rhombus, kite and **trapezium.**

Name of quadrilateral	Diagonals always cut at right angles	Number of lines of symmetry	Order of rotational symmetry
Rectangle			
	Yes		2
		0	2
	Yes	1	
			4

NICCEA

Questions 10 and 11 are on worksheets I1 and I2.

Answers and hints ► page 125

Angles

Types of angle

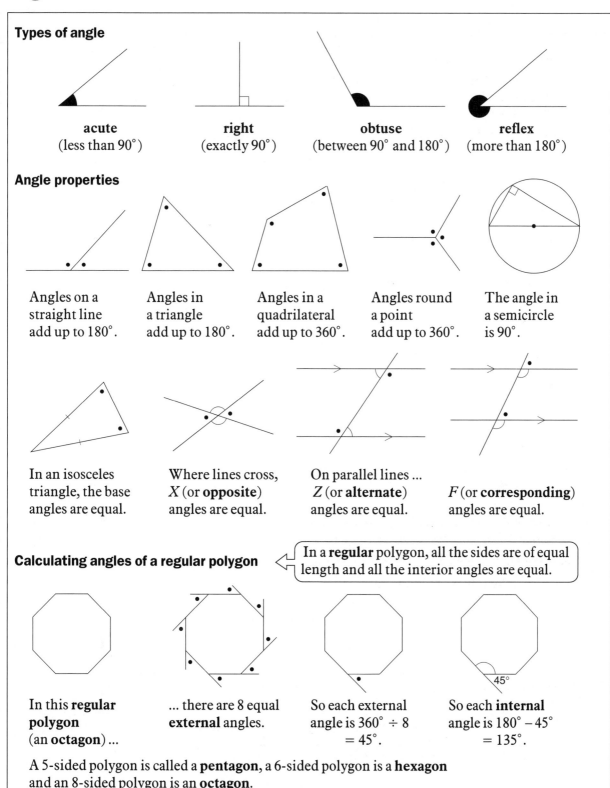

acute
(less than 90°)

right
(exactly 90°)

obtuse
(between 90° and 180°)

reflex
(more than 180°)

Angle properties

Angles on a
straight line
add up to 180°.

Angles in
a triangle
add up to 180°.

Angles in a
quadrilateral
add up to 360°.

Angles round
a point
add up to 360°.

The angle in
a semicircle
is 90°.

In an isosceles
triangle, the base
angles are equal.

Where lines cross,
X (or **opposite**)
angles are equal.

On parallel lines ...
Z (or **alternate**)
angles are equal.

F (or **corresponding**)
angles are equal.

Calculating angles of a regular polygon

In a **regular** polygon, all the sides are of equal
length and all the interior angles are equal.

In this **regular**
polygon
(an **octagon**) ...

... there are 8 equal
external angles.

So each external
angle is 360° ÷ 8
= 45°.

So each **internal**
angle is 180° − 45°
= 135°.

45°

A 5-sided polygon is called a **pentagon**, a 6-sided polygon is a **hexagon**
and an 8-sided polygon is an **octagon**.

None of the diagrams is to scale.

1 (a) In the triangle on the right, work out the size
       of angle a, giving reasons for your answer.

   (b) Work out angle b, giving reasons
       for your answer.

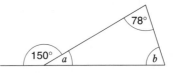

2 ABCDE is a regular pentagon.

   (a) Calculate the sizes of angles
       (i) x
       (ii) y
       (iii) z

   (b) Explain how you know that BE is parallel to CD.

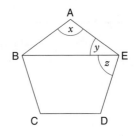

MEG/ULEAC (SMP)

3 (a) Calculate the value of angle p,
       giving reasons for your answer.

   (b) Calculate angle q, giving reasons
       for your answer.

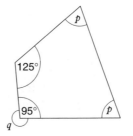

NICCEA

4 Calculate the value of
   (a) x
   (b) y
   (c) z

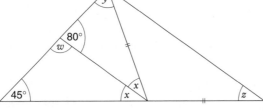

NICCEA

5 PQRS is a parallelogram and
   T is a point on the side PS.
   Angle RQT = 37° and RSP = 122°.

   Write down the values of the angles
   marked a, b, c and d.

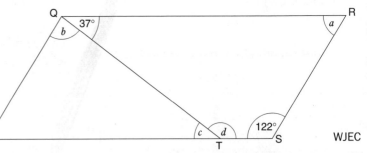

WJEC

6 In the diagrams on the right
   O is the centre of the circle.

   (a) Calculate the size of angle x.

   (b) Calculate the sizes of angles y and z.

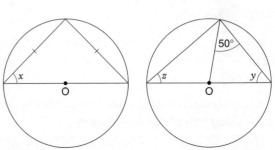

7   The figure shows a regular hexagon ABCDEF
and a regular octagon EFGHIJKL with a
common side FE.

(a) Calculate the size of angle AFE.

(b) Calculate the size of angle GFE.

(c) AF and DE produced meet at X.
GF and LE produced meet at Y.
Calculate the size of angle XFY.

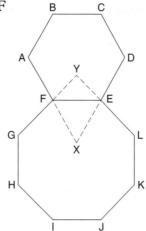

NICCEA

8   Part of the frame of a mountain bike is shown.
AB = AE.
BE is parallel to CD.
Angle BAE is 42°.

(a) Calculate the size of the angle
marked x in the diagram.
Give reasons for your answer.

(b) Angle BED is 74°.
Calculate the size of the angle
marked y in the diagram.
Give reasons for your answer.

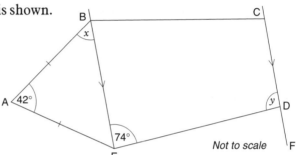

Not to scale

MEG (SMP)

9   ABCD is a rectangle.
CDEF is a rhombus.
AC is parallel to DF.

(a) Find the size of angle CDF.

(b) Find the size of angle DEF.

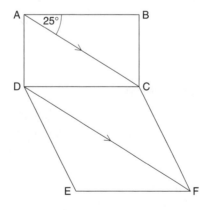

NICCEA

10 O is the centre of the circle and
XY is a tangent to the circle at B.

(a) Find the size of angle BAD.

(b) Find the size of angle CBD.
Give reasons for your answers.

Tangent ► page 54

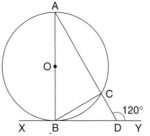

Answers and hints ► page 126

Length, area and volume 1

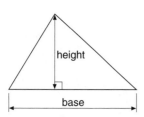

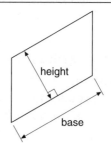

Area of a triangle $= \frac{1}{2} \times$ base $\times$ height   Area of a parallelogram $=$ base $\times$ height

(Notice that the height need not be vertical – just measure it perpendicular to the base.)

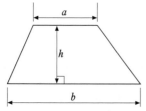

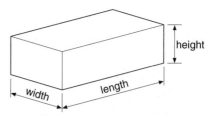

Area of a trapezium $= \frac{1}{2}(a + b)h$ Volume of a cuboid $=$ length $\times$ width $\times$ height

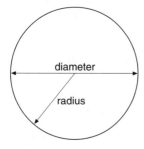

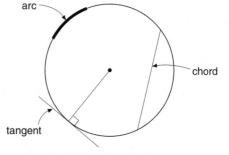

Circumference of a circle $= \pi \times$ diameter
                         $= 2 \times \pi \times$ radius

A tangent touches the circle.
The angle between the tangent and radius is 90°.

The **perimeter** of a shape is the distance round the outside of it.

When you see π in a formula, use the key on your calculator, or use 3·14.

1   By taking suitable measurements, calculate the area of each shape below in cm².

(a)

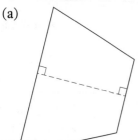

(b)

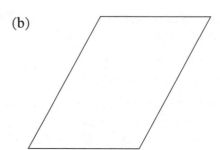

MEG (SMP)

2 This solid is formed from two cuboids.
Calculate its total volume.

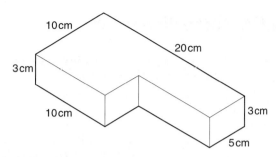

3 A cricket club wants to put a fence round their cricket square.
The square has an area of 900 m².
Calculate the total length of fencing needed to go round the square.

4 A flap door is made for a tent by using
a zip as shown in the diagram.
The zip is made up of a semicircle and
a straight line.
What length of zip is required?
(You may take $\pi = 3\cdot14$.)

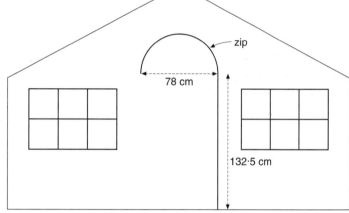

NICCEA

5 Raymond Crescent is in the shape of a semicircle.
The distance from A to B **round the crescent** is 200 m.
How much shorter is it to walk from A to B along the
straight road, rather than round the crescent?

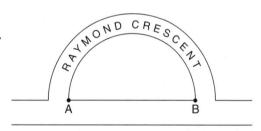

MEG/ULEAC (SMP)

6 Monica has made these measurements of a roll of Sellotape.
The complete roll weighs 56 g.
The tape is 2 cm wide and 66 m long.
The card centre weighs 18 g.

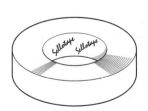

(a) What is the weight in grams of a 1 m length of tape?

(b) The radius of the earth is 6400 km (to 2 significant figures).
    What weight of tape would Monica need
    to wrap once round the equator?
    Give your answer in kg to 2 significant figures.

MEG/ULEAC (SMP)

Answers and hints ► page 127

Representing three dimensions

To show detail in an object, we can draw the **plan** and **elevations** (or views).
All three views must be drawn to the same scale.
Here are the three views for a children's building block.

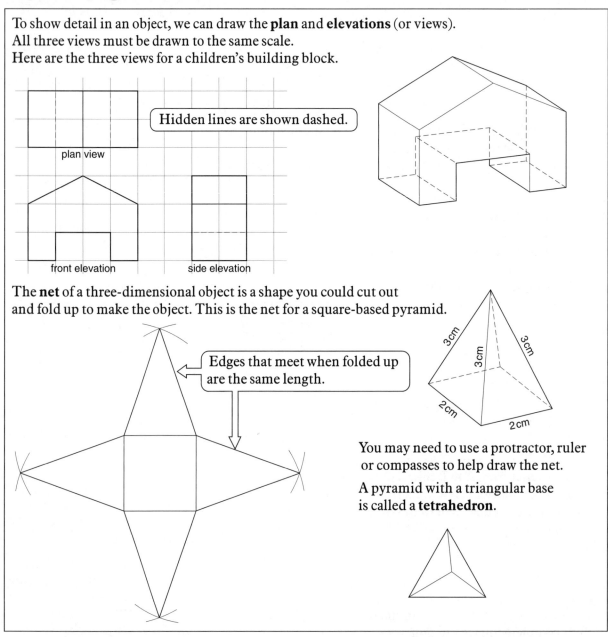

Hidden lines are shown dashed.

plan view

front elevation

side elevation

The **net** of a three-dimensional object is a shape you could cut out
and fold up to make the object. This is the net for a square-based pyramid.

Edges that meet when folded up
are the same length.

3 cm   3 cm   3 cm

2 cm   2 cm

You may need to use a protractor, ruler
or compasses to help draw the net.

A pyramid with a triangular base
is called a **tetrahedron**.

1 The stack in the diagram contains
   six cubes, each of side 2 cm.
   On centimetre squared paper, draw full size
   (a) a front elevation (from F)
   (b) a plan view (from P)
   (c) a side elevation (from S)

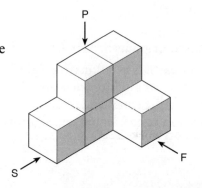

P

S   F

MEG (SMP)

2   The lengths of the edges of a square-based
    pyramid are all 5 cm.

    (a) Draw a full-size net of the pyramid.

    (b) Using measurements from your drawing
        for part (a), draw the elevation of the
        pyramid viewed in the direction of the arrow.

    (c) State the height of the pyramid by taking
        a measurement from your answer to part (b).

MEG/ULEAC (SMP)

3   Chic perfume is sold in bottles.
    Each bottle is a cylinder with diameter 1·5 cm.
    The bottles are packed in cardboard boxes
    like the one on the right.
    Each box contains one bottle.

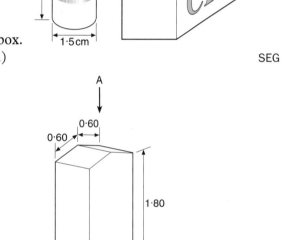

    (a) Copy and complete:
        The minimum dimensions of the box are
        ... cm by ... cm by ... cm.

    (b) On centimetre squared paper draw a net of the box.
        (Do not include flaps for sticking or tucking in.)

SEG

4   The sketch shows a canvas changing tent
    used on the beach.
    The measurements are in metres.
    Apart from the angles formed by the roof,
    all the angles are right-angles.
    On graph paper, use a scale of 4 cm to 1 m
    to draw

    (a) the plan view (from direction A)

    (b) the elevation from direction B

    (c) the elevation from direction C

MEG/ULEAC (SMP)

5   The diagram shows a small wooden box with no lid.
    Its base is a square of side 5 cm.
    The sides are 6 mm thick.

    (a) On centimetre squared paper, draw
        full size the plan of the box.

    (b) From your drawing, measure the length of AB.

    (c) Use this length to help you draw the side view of the
        outside of the box seen from the direction of the arrow.
        The box is 2 cm high.

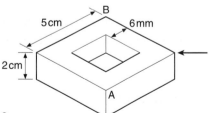

MEG/ULEAC (SMP)

Questions 6, 7 and 8 are on worksheets I3 and I4.

Answers and hints ► page 128

Units, measuring and compound measures

Converting beween 'old' and metric units and vice versa

You need to know all these approximations.

1 pound (lb) is about $\frac{1}{2}$ kg. | So 6 lb is about $6 \times \frac{1}{2}$ kg = 3 kg.

1 inch (in or ") is about 2·5 cm or 25 mm. | So 4 in is about $4 \times 2\cdot5$ cm = 10 cm or 100 mm.

1 foot (ft or ' = 12 inches) is about 30 cm. | So 5 ft is about 5×30 cm = 150 cm.

1 mile is about 1·6 km. | So 15 miles is about $15 \times 1\cdot6$ km = 24 km.

1 pint (pt) is about $\frac{1}{2}$ litre. | So 3 pints is about $3 \times \frac{1}{2}$ litre = $1\frac{1}{2}$ litres.

1 gallon is about 4·5 litres. | So 6 gallons is about $6 \times 4\cdot5$ litres = 26 litres.

1 metre is about 40 inches | So 6 metres is about 240 inches or 20 feet.

1 kilometre is about $\frac{5}{8}$ mile.

1 kilogram is just over 2 pounds. (2·2 lb)

1 litre is just under 2 pints. ($1\frac{3}{4}$ pints)

Converting metric units

1 centimetre (cm) = 10 millimetres (mm) | 1 litre (l) = 100 centilitres (cl)

1 metre (m) = 100 cm | = 1000 millilitres (ml) $\Leftarrow$ 1 ml = 1 cm^3

1 kilometre (km) = 1000 m | 1 cubic metre (m^3) = 1000 litres

1 kilogram (kg) = 1000 grams (g) | 1 tonne = 1000 kg

Examples

$36 \text{ cm} = 36 \times 10 \text{ mm} = 360 \text{ mm}$ | $48 \text{ mm} = 48 \div 10 \text{ cm} = 4\cdot8 \text{ cm}$

$0\cdot6 \text{ m}^3 = 0\cdot6 \times 1000 \text{ litres} = 600 \text{ litres}$ | $2400 \text{ litres} = 2400 \div 1000 \text{ m}^3 = 2\cdot4 \text{ m}^3$

Measuring

Rounding
► page 4

If you measure 'to the nearest cm', then the measurement may be out by $\frac{1}{2}$ cm.
'The length is 4 cm to the nearest cm' means the real length is
between $(4 - \frac{1}{2})$ cm and $(4 + \frac{1}{2})$ cm; or $3\cdot5 \text{ cm} \le \text{real length} < 4\cdot5 \text{ cm}$.

'The weight is 4 kg to the nearest 100 g' means the real weight is between

$(4 \text{ kg} - \frac{1}{2} \times 100 \text{ g})$ and $(4 \text{ kg} + \frac{1}{2} \times 100 \text{ g})$

or $4000 \text{ g} - 50 \text{ g} \le \text{real weight} < 4000 \text{ g} + 50 \text{ g}$

$3950 \text{ g} \le \text{real weight} < 4050 \text{ g}$.

Rates

Time graphs
► page 28

Speed   If I travel 80 km in 5 hours, my average speed is 80 km/5h = 16 km/h.

Density   If a block of metal with volume 450 ml has a density of 7·6 g/ml,
then its mass is $450 \times 7\cdot6 \text{ g} = 3420 \text{ g} = 3\cdot42 \text{ kg}$.

1   For each of the following, write down the one choice from
    the bracket that best completes the sentence.

    (a) The height of an adult is (170 mm, 170 cm, 170 m, 170 km).

    (b) A 16-year-old boy's mass is (60 g, 600 g, 60 kg, 600 kg).

    (c) The area of this page is (450 mm^2, 450 cm^2, 450 m^2, 4·5 mm^2).

    (d) The capacity of a teacup is (200 ml, 2 litres, 20 cm^3, 2 ml).   WJEC

2   How many 20 cl glasses can you fill from a 3-litre bottle?

3   Work out rough metric equivalents of the following.

    (a) 18 in   (b) 4 gallons   (c) 5 feet 6 inches

4   The world long jump record was held by Bob Beamon for twenty years.
    It stood at 8·90 metres.

    Convert 8·90 metres to feet and inches.
    Give your answer to the nearest half inch.

    | 2·54 cm = 1 inch |
    | 12 inches = 1 foot |

                                                                                        MEG/ULEAC (SMP)

5   Sasha and Andy are drawing lines approximately ten centimetres long.
    They take it in turns to draw a line and then measure it.
    Sasha says her line is 0·103 m long. Andy says his line is 9·68 cm long.
    Comment on the units and the degree of accuracy they are using.   MEG/ULEAC (SMP)

6   A stopwatch is accurate to 0·1 seconds.
    In a race, Janet's time on the stopwatch is 12·8 seconds.
    Copy and complete the statement:
    Janet's actual time is between ... seconds and ... seconds.

7   Robin drove 247 miles in 4 hours.
    Work out the average speed in miles per hour.
    Give your answer to the nearest whole number.   ULEAC

8   (a) A train travels between two towns 264 km apart at an average speed
         of 72 km/h. How many minutes does the train take to do the journey?

    (b) A faster train does the journey in 22 minutes less.
         What is the average speed of this train in km/h?   WJEC

9   A recipe needs 8 fluid ounces of milk.
    There are 20 fluid ounces in one pint and one litre is about $1\frac{3}{4}$ pints.

    How many millilitres of milk are needed in the recipe?
    Show your working and give your answer to the nearest 10 millilitres.   MEG/ULEAC (SMP)

10 A large crucible will hold 1·5 litres of molten metal.
    The density of molten gold is 18·7 g/ml.
    What mass of gold will the crucible hold? (Give your answer in kg.)

Answers and hints ► page 129

Transformations

Describing transformations

When you describe a transformation, you need to give enough information to specify it completely.
These are all transformations of A_1 to A_2.

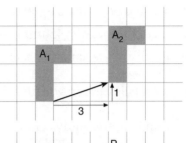

This is a **translation** of **3 across** and **1 up**.
You must give the *across* and *up* distances.

You could give these as a **column vector** $\begin{bmatrix} 3 \\ 1 \end{bmatrix}$.

This is a **rotation** of **90°** anticlockwise, **centre P**.
You need to give the *angle* and the *centre*.

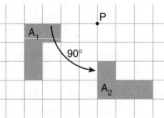

Note that clockwise rotations are negative, anti-clockwise are positive.

It is easiest to find the centre by trying out different points using tracing paper.

This is a **reflection** in the mirror line shown.
You only need to specify the *line* exactly.

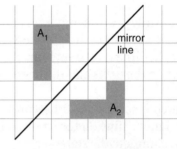

You may have to draw the mirror line or give the equation of the line.
Use tracing paper to check your answer.

This is an **enlargement** with **centre S** and **scale factor 1·5**.
You need to give the *centre* and the *scale factor*.

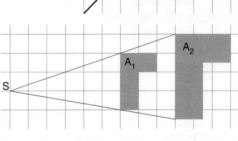

A reduction is just an enlargement with a scale factor between 0 and 1, for example 0·5.

Similarity
► page 62

Strip patterns

One way to make repeating strip patterns is by repeated rotations.

T_1 is rotated 180° about A.

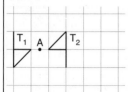

Both T_1 and T_2 are rotated about a different centre, B.

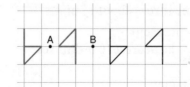

The whole pattern is rotated again about the first centre, A. Then rotate again about B and repeat for ever!

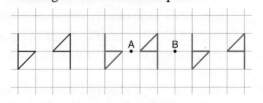

All the questions on transformations are on worksheets I5 to I7.

Answers and hints ► page 130

Loci

A locus is a set of points which fit a particular rule.
For example:

An ant moves so that it is
always 2 cm from the point O.

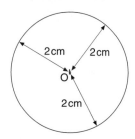

A dog can move so that it is always
5 m or less from the wall of a house.

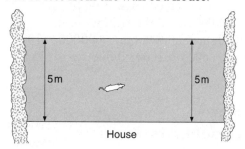

House

A ship sails so that it is the same distance
from lighthouse A as it is from lighthouse B.

The donkey can eat grass inside and
up to 50 cm outside the electric fence.

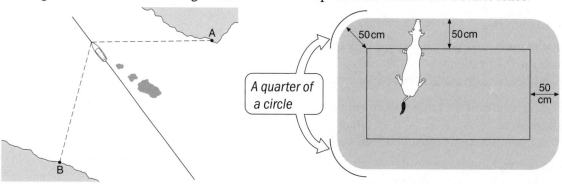

*A quarter of
a circle*

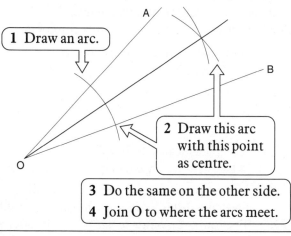

Constructing the locus of a point which is
the same distance from both A and B.

The line is called the **perpendicular
bisector of AB**.

1 With compasses,
draw two equal
arcs, like this.

2 Join where the
arcs meet.

Constructing the locus of a point which is
the same distance from the lines OA and OB.

The line is called the **bisector of angle AOB**.

1 Draw an arc.

2 Draw this arc
with this point
as centre.

3 Do the same on the other side.
4 Join O to where the arcs meet.

All the questions on loci are on worksheets I8 to I11.

Answers and hints ► page 131

Scales and bearings

Metric units ► page 58

Scales on maps

Maps use scales like 1 to 200000 (often written 1 : 200 000).
This means that 1 unit on the map is 200000 units on the ground.

If it is 3 cm between two points on the map,
it is 3×200000 cm on the ground.
3×200000 cm $= 600000$ cm $= 600000 \div 100$ metres
$= 6000$ m $= 6000 \div 1000$ kilometres $= 6$ km

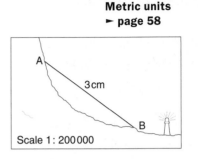

Scale 1 : 200 000

Gradients

Gradient ► pages 24, 38

The **gradient** between two points $= \dfrac{\text{vertical distance between points}}{\text{horizontal distance between points}}$

A gradient of 1 in 4 is the same as $\frac{1}{4} = 0\cdot25$ or 25%.

Enlarging shapes

When a shape is enlarged, we say the new shape
is **similar** to the first one.
You can find the side marked **?** in two ways.

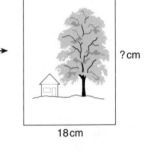

- The rectangle on the left has been enlarged.
  The scale factor must be 18 cm $\div$ 10 cm $= 1\cdot8$.
  So the unknown side must be 15 cm $\times 1\cdot8 = 27$ cm long.

- The two rectangles are similar. So the ratio of the long
  side to the short side in each rectangle must be the same.

  So $\dfrac{15}{10} = \dfrac{?}{18}$ $1\cdot5 = \dfrac{?}{18}$ $? = 27$.

Ratio ► page 14

Bearings

Bearings are measured **clockwise** from North.
They are given in degrees as 3-figure numbers.

'The bearing of P from Q' means you are
standing at Q, looking at P.

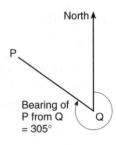

Bearing of
P from Q
$= 305°$

1 (a) A map has scale 1 to 20000.
        What distance on the map would represent 1 km?

   (b) Mary is preparing for her Duke of Edinburgh expedition.
        She has a different map with scale 1 to 50000.
        The route she wants to use measures 30 cm on the map.
        How far will it be in kilometres if she walks this route?

MEG/ULEAC (SMP)

2   The signpost states that the road reaches a gradient
    of 30% or 1 in 3.
    These two gradients are not in fact the same.
    Which of them is steeper?
    Show all your working.

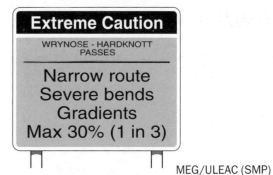

MEG/ULEAC (SMP)

3   Here is a contour map.

    (a) What is the difference in height
        between A and B?

    (b) Find the actual horizontal distance
        between A and B.

    (c) A track is shown from A to B.
        Calculate the average gradient
        of this track.

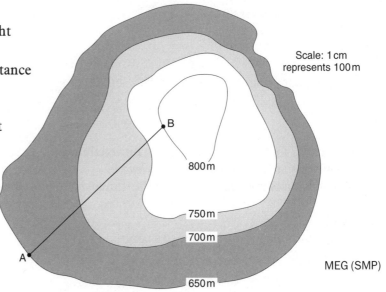

Scale: 1 cm
represents 100 m

800 m

750 m

700 m

650 m

B

A

MEG (SMP)

4    This picture is a rectangle 15 cm wide and 28·5 cm long.

    (a) What is the area of the rectangle?

    The rectangle is enlarged to fit exactly in a frame which is 85·5 cm long.

    (b) (i) What is the scale factor of the enlargement?
        (ii) How wide is the frame?   MEG/ULEAC (SMP)

5   A photographic firm offers enlargements or posters of my 6 × 4 print.
    (All measurements are in inches.)

    (a) I choose the size where the longer side is 10.
        What should be the length of the shorter side in this enlargement?

    (b) The actual advertised size is 10 × 8. Comment on this.   MEG/ULEAC (SMP)

6   A page of a book is exactly 169 mm wide and 238 mm long.
    When reduced on a photocopier, the copy is 119 mm wide.
    Find the length of the copy, to the nearest millimetre.   MEG/ULEAC (SMP)

Questions 7, 8 and 9 are on worksheets I12, I13 and I14.

Answers and hints ► page 132

Length, area and volume 2

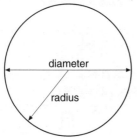

diameter

radius

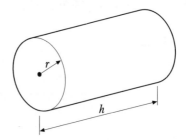

r

h

Area of a circle $= \pi \times (\text{radius})^2 = \pi r^2$

Volume of a cylinder $= \pi r^2 h$

Volume of prism $=$ area of cross-section $\times$ length

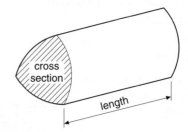

cross section

length

You can check formulas by considering **dimensions**.
The dimension of perimeters is always *length*.
The dimension of areas is *length²*, and the dimension of volumes is *length³*.

Example
Could the formula for the volume of a cone be $2\pi rh$?

h

r

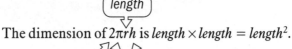

length

The dimension of $2\pi rh$ is *length* $\times$ *length* $=$ *length²*.

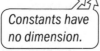

Constants have no dimension.

length

A volume must have dimension *length³*, so the formula cannot be correct.
(The actual formula is $\frac{1}{3}\pi r^2 h$.)

1   A new reservoir has a circular concrete wall.
    The diameter of the reservoir is 180 m.

    (a) Calculate the surface area of the
        water in the reservoir.

    (b) When the reservoir is full,
        the average depth of water is 12 m.
        Calculate the capacity of the reservoir in m³.

    (c) The reservoir serves a population of 12 000.
        On average, each person uses 120 litres of water a day.
        How many days would a full reservoir last
        if there was no water going into it?
        (1 m³ $= 1000$ litres.)

2 On the right is a sketch of an ellipse.
It is symmetrical about both axes.

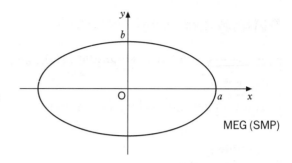

(a) Which of the following could possibly be
an expression for its area?

$$2\pi\sqrt{(ab)} \quad \pi(a + b) \quad \tfrac{1}{2}\pi(a^2 + b^2) \quad \pi ab \quad \pi(ab)^2$$

(b) Explain how you made your choice.

MEG (SMP)

3 The diagram represents a triangular prism
whose ends are right-angled triangles.

(a) Write down the number of faces
of the prism.

(b) (i) Calculate the area of triangle ABC.
(ii) Calculate the volume of the prism.
(iii) Calculate the total surface area
of the prism.

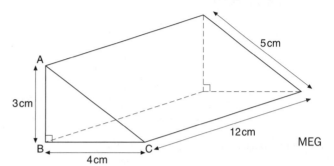

MEG

4 A tray is circular, with a rim as shown in the diagram.
The tray is horizontal.

(a) What is the area of the base of the tray?

(b) John spilt half a litre of orange juice onto the tray.
What was the depth of the liquid on the tray?
Give your answer to the nearest millimetre.

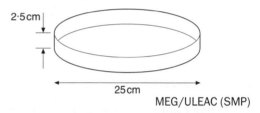

MEG/ULEAC (SMP)

5

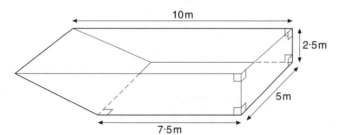

A hole is made for a swimming pool.
The dimensions of the hole are shown
in the sketch.
Calculate the volume of earth removed.

6 A length of softwood moulding has a cross-section
consisting of a square with a quarter of a circle removed.
The measurements are in centimetres.

(a) What is the radius of the circle?

(b) Calculate the area of the cross-section of the moulding.

(c) The softwood weighs $0.8\,\text{g/cm}^3$.
What is the weight of a 3 m length of this moulding?

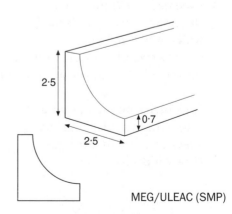

MEG/ULEAC (SMP)

Answers and hints ► page 133

65

Pythagoras' rule

Pythagoras' rule works for any 90° (right-angled) triangle.

$$a^2 + b^2 = c^2$$

c is the longest side, called the **hypotenuse**.

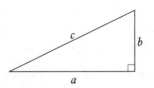

Example 1
Find the length of c.

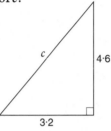

First write down the rule. $a^2 + b^2 = c^2$
Replace a and b: $3{\cdot}2^2 + 4{\cdot}6^2 = c^2$
$$10{\cdot}24 + 21{\cdot}16 = c^2$$
$$31{\cdot}4 = c^2$$
So $c = \sqrt{31{\cdot}4}$
$$= 5{\cdot}567...$$

c is 5·6 cm long (to 2 s.f.)

Example 2
Find the length of AC.

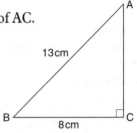

Suppose AC is b cm long.
First write down the rule. $a^2 + b^2 = c^2$
Replace the values you know: $8^2 + b^2 = 13^2$
$$64 + b^2 = 169$$
$$b^2 = 169 - 64 = 105$$
So $b = \sqrt{105} = 10{\cdot}246...$
AC is 10·2 cm long (to 3 s.f.)

Significant figures ► page 6

---

1   When I built my greenhouse, I first had to lay the base
which was a rectangle 3·15 m by 2·43 m.
To check it was a rectangle, the instructions told me
to measure the diagonals and make sure they were
the same length.
Calculate how long they should be.

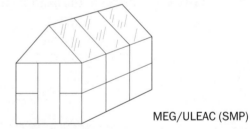

MEG/ULEAC (SMP)

2   To break the world record, 813 pupils had
to be tied in a 'human chain'.
In a practice, 100 pupils made a straight line
which was 72 m long.
Could a **straight** line of 813 pupils fit on
the school field? Show all your working.

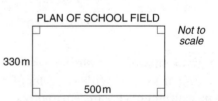

MEG/ULEAC (SMP)

3   A 13-inch computer monitor measures 13 inches
across the diagonal of the screen.
The screen is 8 inches high.
How wide is it?

4   Passengers on coaches sometimes get bored,
so a travel firm gives its passengers a small
thin wallet at the start of a journey.
The wallet has square corners and measures
110 mm by 150 mm.
Inside is a puzzle book and a pencil.
The pencil is 175 mm long.
Use calculation to show that the pencil
will fit in the wallet.

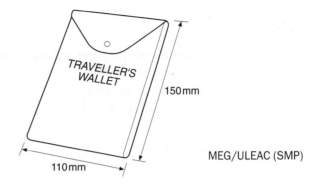

MEG/ULEAC (SMP)

5   It is possible to make an equilateral triangle by folding a circle
as shown in the diagram.

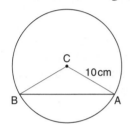 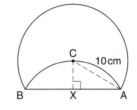 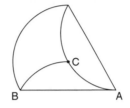 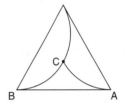

C is the centre of the circle, X is the mid-point of AB.
Angle CXA is 90°. The radius is 10 cm.

(a) Explain why CX is 5 cm.

(b) (i) Work out the length of AX.
    (ii) Work out the length of a side of the equilateral triangle.   MEG/ULEAC (SMP)

6   *Not to scale*

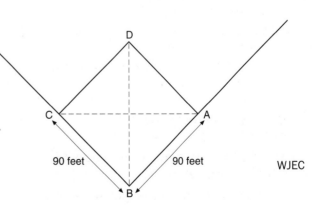

The diagram shows a square OXYZ with
sides of length 8 cm.
It is drawn in a semicircle with diameter AB
and O is the mid-point of AB.
Calculate the radius of the semicircle.   WJEC

7   In the diagram, ABCD represents part
of a baseball pitch in the shape of a square
with sides of length 90 feet.
The batter stands at B and the pitcher at
a point P on BD such that BP is 60·5 feet.

(a) Calculate the length of CA, correct to 1 d.p.

(b) Is the pitcher closer to D than B?
    Give a reason for your answer.   WJEC

Answers and hints ► page 134

Trigonometry

In a right-angled triangle we give special names to the sides.
The longest side is the **hypotenuse**.
The other side next to an angle we know is the **adjacent** side.
The third side is the side **opposite** the angle we know.

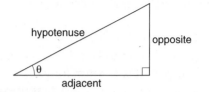

$$\sin \theta = \frac{\text{opposite}}{\text{hypotenuse}} \qquad \cos \theta = \frac{\text{adjacent}}{\text{hypotenuse}} \qquad \tan \theta = \frac{\text{opposite}}{\text{adjacent}}$$

In a trigonometric problem you will always be given two values,
and need to find a third. Pick the formula that links these three things,
and substitute what you know into it. Then solve the equation you get.

Example 1
Find the length AB.

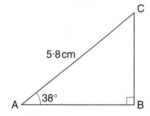

Example 2
A pylon is 36 m tall and is 24 m from a point P
on the ground. Find the angle of elevation *e* of
the top of the pylon from P.

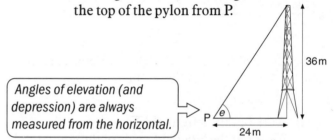

*Angles of elevation (and
depression) are always
measured from the horizontal.*

You know an angle and the hypotenuse.
You want the adjacent side.
So you must use $\cos \theta = \dfrac{\text{adj}}{\text{hyp}}$

$$\cos 38° = AB \div 5{\cdot}8$$
$$5{\cdot}8 \times \cos 38° = AB$$
$$AB = 4{\cdot}5704... = 4{\cdot}6 \text{ (to 1 d.p.)}$$

On most calculators, press

to work this out.

You know the side opposite the angle,
and the side adjacent to the angle.
So you must use $\tan \theta = \dfrac{\text{opp}}{\text{adj}}$

$$\tan e = 36 \div 24 = 1{\cdot}5$$
$$e = \text{inv} \tan 1{\cdot}5$$
$$= 56{\cdot}30...° = 56° \text{ (to the nearest degree)}$$

On calculators, you usually press

to work this out.

You often need to use Pythagoras' rule to solve trigonometric problems.

Pythagoras' rule
► page 66

None of the diagrams is drawn to scale.

1   A cliff railway climbs at an angle of 63°.
    The track is 120 m long.

    (a) Work out BC (the height of the cliff).

    (b) Work out the distance AB.

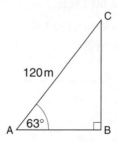

2 A farmyard gate is 1·8 m wide.
The diagonal bar makes an angle of 31°
with the bottom rail.

(a) What is the height of the gate?

(b) What is the length of the diagonal bar?

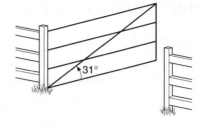

MEG/ULEAC (SMP)

3 The diagram shows a side view of the assembly hall and the humanities
block at Lucy's school. The distance between the buildings, PR, is 14·2 m.

MEG (SMP)

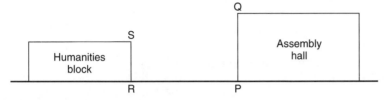

Lucy measures the angle of elevation of Q from R.
She finds this angle is 31°.
Calculate the height, PQ, of the assembly hall.

4 The diagram shows a truss used in
making the roof of a house.

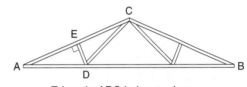

(a) Calculate the angle of the roof,
marked a.

Triangle ABC is isosceles.
AD = 2·29 m, ED = 1·27 m.

(b) AB is 6·45 m.
What is the vertical distance
of C above AB?

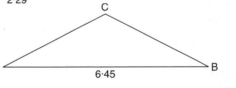

MEG/ULEAC (SMP)

5 A ship sails due south (180°) from the port at A
for a distance of 10 miles to a point B.
It then sails for 20 miles on a bearing of S35°E (145°)
to C, before finally sailing 8 miles due east (090°)
to the port at D. Calculate

(a) the length of BX

(b) the length of XC

(c) the bearing of A from D.

Bearings ► page 62

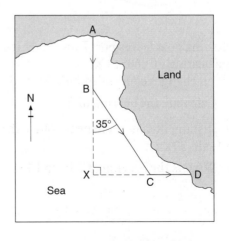

WJEC

Answers and hints ► page 135

Mixed shape, space and measures

None of the diagrams is drawn to scale.

1

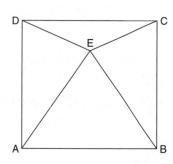

The diagram shows a square ABCD and an equilateral triangle AEB.

(a) Calculate angle DAE.

(b) (i) Explain why AD = AE.
    (ii) Calculate angle AED.

(c) Calculate angle DEC.

MEG

2 ABC is a triangle and AD is the perpendicular from A to BC.
AB = 11 cm, BD = 9 cm and DC = 7 cm

Calculate: (a) the length of AD

(b) the area of triangle ABC

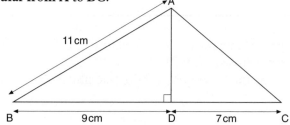

WJEC

3

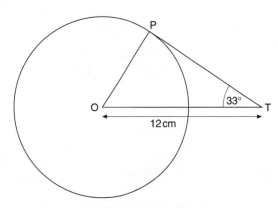

The point P lies on a circle which has centre O.
PT is a tangent to the circle.

(a) Explain why angle OPT = 90°.

(b) Calculate, correct to 3 significant figures, the radius of the circle.

MEG

4 A fishing boat leaves port P and sails 15 km on a bearing of 060° to X.
It then changes course through 90° and sails 15 km to Y.

(a) Calculate the bearing of Y from P.

The fishing boat now changes course through 90° once more and sails 30 km to Z.

(b) What is the bearing of Z from P?

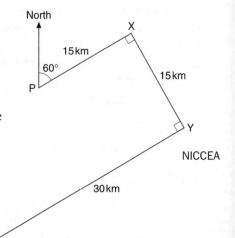

NICCEA

70

5 An athletics track has two straights, each 90 metres long, and two semicircles, each 110 metres long.

(a) Calculate the total length of the track.

(b) Calculate the radius of the semicircle.

(c) Lou runs 100 metres in 13·3 seconds. Calculate her speed in metres per second.

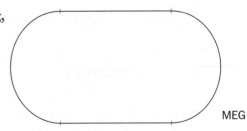

MEG

6 The diagram shows a repeating pattern made by a car tyre. The tyre is 185 mm wide.

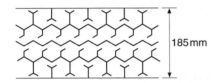

185 mm

(a) What is the scale of the diagram?

(b) Find the period of the repeating pattern on the full size tyre.

MEG/ULEAC (SMP)

7 Jessica's car travels a distance of 750 m in a straight line up the hill. The angle of inclination of the hill is 14° to the horizontal AC.

(a) Calculate the vertical height BC. Give your answer to the nearest metre.

Jessica's car travelled up the hill at an average speed of 60 kilometres per hour.

(b) Calculate the time the car took to travel from A to B. Give your answer in seconds.

B

750 m

14°

A

C

ULEAC

8

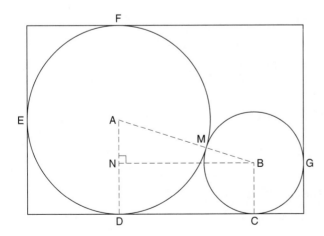

A circular disc, centre A, of radius 9 cm touches another circular disc, centre B, of radius 5 cm at the point M. The discs also touch the sides of a rectangle at C, D, E, F and G as shown in the diagram.

(a) Find the length of AB.

(b) N is the foot of the perpendicular from B to AD. Find the length of AN.

(c) Calculate the length of NB.

(d) Find the length and breadth of the outer rectangle.

WJEC

9 (a) Draw accurately a regular pentagon with its vertices on the circumference of a circle of radius 6 cm.

(b) Use measurements from your drawing to calculate the area of the part of the circle which is not inside the pentagon.

MEG/ULEAC (SMP)

10 A 150 m length of aluminium wire has a circular cross-section of diameter 1·8 mm.

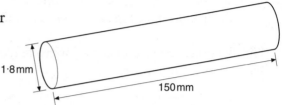

(a) What is the radius of the wire in cm?

(b) Calculate the volume of the wire in cm³.

(c) 1 cm³ of the wire has a mass of 2·69 g. Calculate the mass of the 150 m length of wire in kg.

WJEC

11

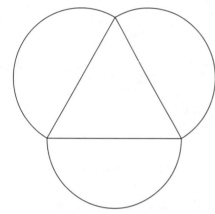

The diagram represents a window.
The window has four pieces of glass.
One piece is an equilateral triangle of side 40 cm.
The other three pieces are semicircles.

(a) Calculate the height, in cm, of the equilateral triangle.

(b) Calculate the area, in cm², of the equilateral triangle.

(c) Calculate the area, in cm², of one semicircle.

(d) Calculate the total area, in cm², of glass in the window.

The lines in the diagram represent strips of lead.

(e) Calculate the total length, in cm, of lead strip in the window.

ULEAC

12 An aircraft takes off from a point A at the end of a runway at a speed of 150 m.p.h. It remains at this speed whilst it climbs at an angle of 20° for one minute until it reaches a point B. This point B is directly above a point C on the coastline.

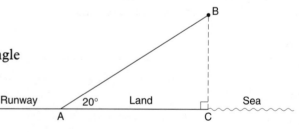

(a) AB represents the distance that the aircraft has travelled in its climb in one minute. Show clearly how to calculate that this distance is 2·5 miles.

Calculate, in miles, correct to 2 decimal places,

(b) the height, BC, the aircraft is above the coastline

(c) the distance, AC, from the runway to the coast.

WJEC

Answers and hints ► page 137

HANDLING DATA

Surveys

A survey should test a theory or **hypothesis** or should have some other clear purpose.

In a survey you can record each person's replies on a **questionnaire**. This is sometimes called a **data collection sheet**.

It is sometimes easier to record everybody's replies on one **tally chart**.

Car Colour	Tally	Frequency
Red	ЖНТ III	8
Black	ЖНТ ЖНТ	9
Blue	III	3
White	II	2
Other	ЖНТ ЖНТ	10

You must be careful with the questions you ask, especially if you want to **analyse** your results in a table or a chart:

- The meaning of the questions should be clear.

- They should allow a 'yes' or 'no' answer, or they should give people a choice from just a few common answers.

- They should not try to persuade people to answer in a particular way. Questions that try to do this are **biased**. They are sometimes called **leading questions**.

The people you ask should be **representative** of the kind of people you are interested in. If you want to find out what adults in general think about gambling, it's no good asking people who are coming out of a betting shop. That would be a **biased sample** of adults.

1 Say whether each of these questions is suitable for a questionnaire. If you think not, explain why.

   (a) What do you think of the shopping facilities in the centre of town?

   (b) Do you agree that the ugly old shops in the high street should be pulled down and replaced by lovely modern ones?

   (c) If you have been down East Street recently did you buy anything in any of the shops there?

   (d) Tick one box to show how much you spent on shopping last Saturday:

   £0 to £19·99 ☐   £20 to £39·99 ☐   £40 or more ☐

2 The Council want to find out what facilities people of all ages would like in a new leisure centre that they are planning. Comment on the reliability of the information that they would get by each of these methods.

   (a) They interview 200 people chosen at random coming out of the old swimming pool.

   (b) They choose 200 people at random from the phone book and interview them over the phone between 9 a.m. and 5 p.m.

   (c) They interview a boy and a girl under 10, a male and a female teenager, a man and a woman between 20 and 60 and a male and a female pensioner.

Answers and hints ► page 139

Timetables and calendars

Questions on times and dates are usually straightforward, so long as you check carefully.
But they can sometimes be turned into a challenge, like question 3!

1 This is part of a train timetable.

(a) Look at the train that leaves Watford Junction at 0756.
What time does it get to Wolverhampton?

(b) Look at the train that leaves London Euston at 0840.
How long does this train take to get to Birmingham International?

(c) Sajid walks to Coventry station.
He gets there at quarter past eight in the morning.
 (i) What time does the next train to Birmingham New Street depart?
 (ii) How long does Sajid have to wait?

London ➡ West Midlands				
Mondays to Fridays				
London Euston	0635	0740	0840	0940
Watford Junction	0652	0756	0856	0956
Coventry	0752	0849	0949	1049
Birmingham International	0803	0901	1001	1101
Birmingham New Street	0823	0918	1018	1118
Wolverhampton	0844	0941	1041	1141

MEG (SMP)

2 This table shows distances on the railway line from Aberystwyth to Shrewsbury.

Stations on the line	Distance from Aberystwyth (miles)
Aberystwyth	0
Borth	8
Dovey Junction	17
Machynlleth	20
Caersws	42
Newtown	48
Welshpool	62
Shrewsbury	82

Copy this distance chart. ⇨
Use the information in
the table to complete it.

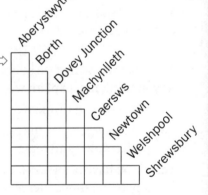

3

⇦ These are the first six months of the year from an old calendar.
But they have been **mixed up**.
Sort them out by making a table like this
and filling in the letters. ⇨

Month	Letter
January	
February	
March	
April	
May	
June	

NICCEA

Answers and hints ► page 139

74

Interpreting tables

You may have to compare quantities, get a total of a column or row, or work out percentages.

If you have to work out a percentage, study the table carefully to make sure you know what quantity you are working out a percentage of.

Finding what percentage one quantity is of another quantity
► page 10

1   The table shows the destination of all 16-year-olds leaving school in 1989, 1990 and 1991.

	Total	Education	Youth training	Job	Unemployed	Not known
1989		300000	135000	120000	30000	55000
1990	580000	305000	100000	100000	40000	35000
1991	570000	350000	85000	55000	50000	30000

(a) What was the total number of 16-year-olds leaving school in 1989?

(b) What percentage of 16-year-olds leaving in 1991 was unemployed?

(c) (i) What was the increase in the number in education from 1989 to 1991?
     (ii) What percentage increase is this?

MEG/ULEAC (SMP)

2

	12 months APR 18%			36 months APR 18%		
Amount of loan £	Monthly repayment £	Total interest £	Total to repay £	Monthly repayment £	Total interest £	Total to repay £
500	45.56	46.72	546.72	17.74	138.64	638.64
600	54.63	55.56	655.56	21.29	166.44	766.44
700	63.73	64.76	764.76	24.84	194.24	894.24
800	72.84	74.08	874.08	28.39	222.04	1022.04
900	81.94	83.28	983.28	31.94	249.84	1149.84
1000	91.05	92.60	1092.60	35.49	277.64	1277.64
1100	100.15	101.80	1201.80	39.04	305.44	1405.44
1200	109.26	111.12	1311.12	42.58	332.88	1532.88
1300	118.36	120.32	1420.32	46.13	360.68	1660.68
1400	127.46	129.52	1529.52	49.68	388.48	1788.48
1500	136.57	138.84	1638.84	53.23	416.28	1916.28

(a) Mark can afford to have a loan if the monthly repayment is not more than £50. What is the largest loan he can afford?

(b) Marion takes out a loan of £900.
    What percentage of her total repayment is interest if
    (i) she repays it over 12 months?
    (ii) she repays it over 36 months?

(c) Peter takes out a £700 loan at a lower rate of interest than the one for this table. He repays it over 12 months and the total interest is £62.04. What is his monthly repayment?

Answers and hints ► page 140

Mode, mean, median and range

Separate items of data

Suppose you have been given these fifteen items of data:

13 10 10 9 13 9 11 13 12 10 9 12 11 13 13

The **mode** is the value that occurs most frequently.

To find the **mean** add up the items and divide by the number of items.

Total = 168   Mean = 168 ÷ 15 = 11·2

If you put the items in order
the one in the middle is the **median**.

If there are an even number of data items,
there will be **two** items in the middle.
Add them up and divide by 2 to get the median.

9 9 9 10 10 10 11 11 12 12 13 13 13 13 13

To find the **range**, look for the smallest and the largest value.
Calculate the difference between them.
        Range = 13 − 9 = 4

Data in a table

Our fifteen items of data
could be recorded in a table.

Value	9	10	11	12	13
Frequency	3	3	2	2	5

You can work out that the middle (eighth) item is in here,
so 11 must be the median.

This shows that 13
is the mode.

To calculate the total of all the data items you can work out $(9 \times 3) + (10 \times 3) + ...$
Then you divide by the number of items to get the mean.

1   At a school parents' evening, a teacher spoke to 16 parents.
    She recorded the time, in minutes, that she spoke with each parent as follows.

    8 11 4 7 6 6 9 5 11 6 8 7 4 8 5 7

(a) (i) Calculate the total time, in minutes, that she spent speaking to parents.
    (ii) Calculate the mean of the 16 times.

(b) The teacher was at the parents' evening for $2\frac{1}{2}$ hours.
    For how many minutes was she not speaking to parents?

MEG

2   The table shows the number of runs scored by
    two cricket teams in their last 6 matches.

Whitecross	Newtown
184	153
106	149
215	165
109	180
196	157
156	171

(a) The mean number of runs scored by Whitecross is 161.
    Work out the mean number of runs scored by Newtown.

(b) The range of the runs scored by Newtown is 31.
    What is the range of the runs scored by Whitecross?

(c) Make two comments comparing the performances of the two teams.

MEG (SMP)

3   This table shows the average daily maximum temperature in °C
    for each month in Manchester and Vladivostock.

Month	J	F	M	A	M	J	J	A	S	O	N	D
Manchester	8	8	10	12	17	19	21	21	18	14	10	8
Vladivostock	⁻9	⁻6	1	8	12	18	22	25	21	12	3	⁻6

   (a) The mean of the temperatures for Manchester is 13·8°C.   **Adding negative numbers**
       Work out the mean of the temperatures for Vladivostock.   ► **page 7**

   (b) Work out the range of the temperatures for each city.

   (c) Which city has the greater variation in average daily maximum temperature?

4   These are the weights in kilograms of the vegetable marrows
    entered for a village competition.

       3·2   4·8   3·7   4·3   2·9   5·2   3·6   4·7   5·1   4·9   5·0

    Give the median weight.

5   A railway company records the time that each train arrives at Witton Station.
    Each time is compared with the expected time of arrival.
    The diagram shows the number of minutes that trains were late one Thursday.

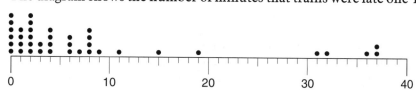

   (a) What is the median number of minutes late?

   (b) Work out the mean number of minutes late.   MEG (SMP)

6   Garth is doing a survey of the number of
    children in families.
    The table shows the results for his own class.

Number of children	1	2	3	4	5
Number of families	4	7	6	5	2

   (a) What is the mode for these data?

   (b) Calculate the mean number of children in families for Garth's class.

7   The frequency table shows the temperature at midnight for
    a ski resort in December 1992.

Temperature °C	⁻3	⁻2	⁻1	0	1	2	3	4	5	6	7
Number of nights	2	3	4	3	4	2	3	6	3	0	1

   (a) State the modal temperature.

   (b) Find the median temperature.

   (c) Calculate the mean temperature.
       Give your answer correct to 1 decimal place.   ULEAC

Answers and hints ► **page 140**

Frequency distributions 1

A **frequency distribution** shows how frequently certain values occur in a set of data.
You can use a table or a diagram like this to show the distribution.

Number of goals	Number of games
0	3
1	2
2	4
3	2
4	1

This means that the team scored 4 goals in only one of the games.

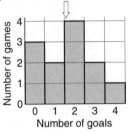

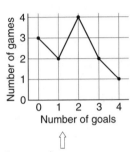

Instead of bars, you could use vertical lines or joined-up points.
(A frequency diagram with joined-up points is sometimes called a **frequency polygon**.)

A **pie chart** is another way of displaying a frequency distribution.

Pie charts
► **page 80 or 81**

Sometimes you need to put data into groups, with a range of values in each group.

Age	Tally	Frequency
0–19	⊦⊦⊦⊦ |||	8
20–39	⊦⊦⊦⊦ ⊦⊦⊦⊦ |||	13
40–59	⊦⊦⊦⊦ ⊦⊦⊦⊦ ⊦⊦⊦⊦		16
60–79	⊦⊦⊦⊦ ||||	9
		46

When you fill in a frequency table from a set of data, check that the total of the frequency column agrees with the number of data items that you were given.

Mode ► page 76

1   Rita and Rakesh are conducting a survey on absence in their school.
They use class registers and record the number of absences for each student.

Here are their results for form 11A.

(a) What is the mode of these results?

0	24	1	16	0	11	5	0
2	5	9	0	21	0	22	7
10	0	27	3	7	8	0	4
0	13	0	7	11	18	1	14

(b) Copy and complete this frequency table for these results.

(c) (i) How many students were in form 11A?

(ii) How many students in form 11A had 10 or more absences?

Number of absences	Tally	Frequency
0–4		
5–9		
10–14		
15–19		
20–24		
25 and above		

MEG/ULEAC (SMP)

78

2 The bar chart comes from a survey of
   20 secondary schools.

   (a) How many schools have 6 maths teachers?

   (b) How many schools have 8 or more maths teachers?

   (c) What fraction of schools have
       8 or more maths teachers?

   (d) How many maths teachers are there altogether in
       the 20 schools?

   (e) What is the mean number of maths teachers
       in a school?

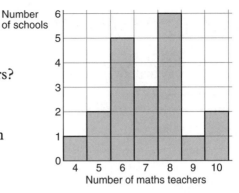

Mean ► page 76

3 These are the heights in centimetres of a class of 30 pupils.

   154   167   163   148   143   169   155   179   153   173
   167   164   151   160   172   160   161   150   164   178
   156   155   165   152   164   166   163   170   172   169

   (a) Copy this table and complete it
       for the heights.

   (b) How many pupils were
       160 cm or taller?

   (c) On worksheet I15, draw a
       frequency diagram to show
       the distribution of heights.

Height (cm)	Tally	Number of pupils
140–149		
150–159		
160–169		
170–179		

4 Some pupils in a school recorded how long
   it took them to travel to school.
   This frequency diagram shows their results.

   (a) How many pupils took part?

   (b) How many pupils recorded less than 10 minutes?

   (c) How many recorded less than 20 minutes?

   (d) How many recorded 20 minutes or more?

   (e) What is the modal time interval?

   The teachers also were asked
   how long they took to travel to school.   3   11   8   38   7   35   19   15   5   31
   These were their times in minutes.   ⇨   33   12   21   4   23   16   36   14   6   7

   (f) Copy and complete this table for
       the teachers' times.

   (g) On worksheet I15, draw a frequency
       diagram for the teachers' times.

Time to the nearest minute	Tally	Frequency
0–9		
10–19		
20–29		
30–39		

Answers and hints ► page 141

Pie charts (using a pie chart scale)

Percentages can be represented as 'slices' of a pie chart.

The simplest way to draw pie chart slices or measure them is to use a pie chart scale.
Each small division on the scale is 1%.

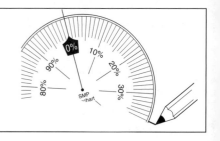

1   Sanjay asked the year 10 pupils at Parkfield School
    which was their favourite sport.
    His results are shown here.

    (a) Draw and label a pie chart to show his results.

Sport	Percentage
Football	21
Basketball	19
Hockey	35
Netball	20
Other	5

    (b) Marie asked the year 10 pupils in
        Whitefield School which was their
        favourite sport.
        Her results are shown in this pie chart.

        There were 225 pupils in year 10 in
        Whitefield School.
        How many replied 'Basketball'?

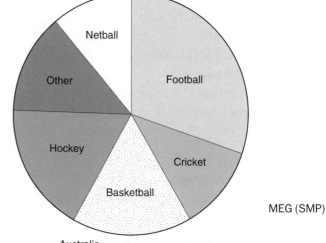

MEG (SMP)

2   The Earth's land surface is
    divided up into seven
    continents. This pie chart shows
    the percentage of the Earth's
    land surface covered by each
    continent.

    (a) Which continent has the
        largest area?

    (b) Use a pie chart scale to find
        the percentage of the Earth's
        land surface that is covered
        by Africa.

    MEG/ULEAC (SMP)

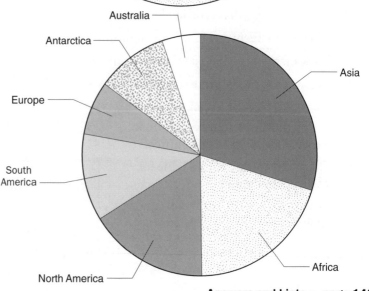

Answers and hints ► page 142

Pie charts (using a protractor)

The angles of the slices of a pie chart are proportional to the numbers they represent.

A bicycle costs £225. The table shows how the price is made up.

Item	Price (£)
Materials	135
Labour	40
Sales	25
Overheads	15
Profit	10
Total	225

Proportion
► **page 14**

£225 is represented by the total angle at the centre of the pie. So £1 is represented by $360° \div 225 = 1·6°$. £135, the value of the materials part of the price, would be represented by a slice with an angle of

$$(135 \times 1·6°) = 216°$$

The rest of the angles are worked out in the same way.

Item	Angle (°)
Materials	216
Labour	64
Sales	40
Overheads	24
Profit	16
Total	360

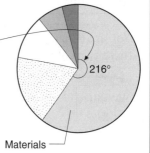

If you know how much the whole pie represents, you can work out how much each slice represents. 108 cars were sold at an auction. This pie chart represents the countries where they were made. 360° represents 108 cars. So 1° represents

$$108 \div 360 = 0·3 \text{ cars}.$$

The slice representing cars from France measures 80°, so the number of French cars is $80 \times 0·3 = 24$.

You can use a similar method if you know the angle of any one slice and how much it represents.

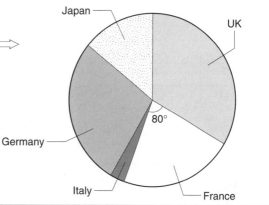

1 Susie sold the number of sandwiches shown in the table.

Represent this information on a pie chart. Show clearly how you work out the angles.

Ham	50
Beef	40
Cheese	60
Tuna	30

2 A car dealer sells Standard, De-Luxe and Super cars. The pie chart represents the number of cars the dealer sold in 1990.

(a) The dealer sold 56 De-Luxe cars. Calculate the total number of cars sold.

(b) The dealer sold three times as many Standard cars as Super cars. Calculate the angle of the sector which represents the number of Standard cars sold.

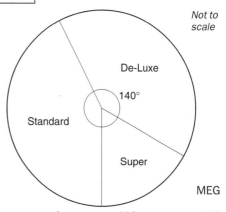

Not to scale

MEG

Answers and hints ► page 142

81

Frequency distributions 2

The **mid-interval** method lets you calculate an estimate of the **mean** from a frequency distribution that has **grouped data**.

The mid-interval value is the value in the middle of the group.
Work it out by adding the upper and lower limits for the group and dividing by two: $(3 + 4) \div 2 = 3{\cdot}5$

The method works out the mean that you would get if all the items in each group had the mid-interval value of their group.
They don't usually, but the method works quite well because values above the mid-interval value are usually balanced by values below it.

You are usually given these two columns.

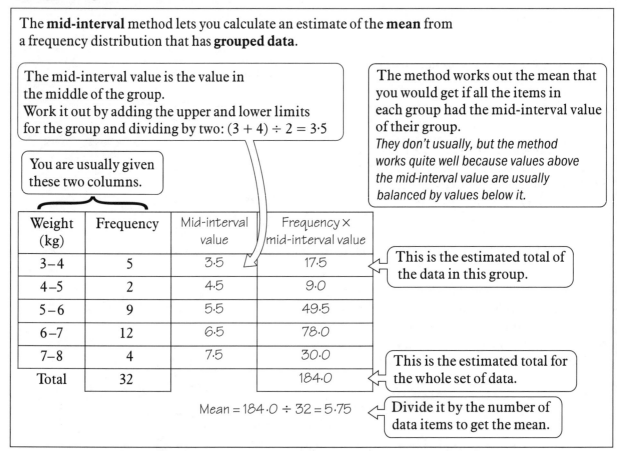

Weight (kg)	Frequency	Mid-interval value	Frequency × mid-interval value	
3–4	5	3·5	17·5	This is the estimated total of the data in this group.
4–5	2	4·5	9·0	
5–6	9	5·5	49·5	
6–7	12	6·5	78·0	
7–8	4	7·5	30·0	
Total	32		184·0	This is the estimated total for the whole set of data.

Mean = 184·0 ÷ 32 = 5·75 — Divide it by the number of data items to get the mean.

1 Mrs James has two daughters, Ann and Barbara.
She asks them to record the length of the next 50 telephone calls they each make.
The following table gives the length, in minutes, for the 50 calls made by Ann.

Length of call (minutes)	Frequency		
0–5	8		
5–10	12		
10–15	14		
15–20	10		
20–25	6		

(a) Copy the table and use the method of mid-interval values to calculate an estimate of the mean length of Ann's telephone calls.

(b) The graph on worksheet I16 shows the data for Barbara's calls.
On the same diagram draw a frequency polygon for Ann's calls.

(c) Use the data collected to compare Ann's and Barbara's use of the telephone.

MEG (SMP)

2 The frequency table gives information about the length, in millimetres, of 40 worms.

(a) Use the method of mid-interval values to estimate the mean length of the worms.

(b) On worksheet I16, draw a frequency diagram to show the information in the table.

Length of worm (mm)	Frequency		
0–40	4		
40–80	25		
80–120	8		
120–160	2		
160–200	1		

MEG (SMP)

3 The speed of 100 cars on a motorway was recorded. This is the distribution.

Speed, s (m.p.h.)	Number of cars		
$40 \leq s < 50$	2		
$50 \leq s < 60$	15		
$60 \leq s < 70$	34		
$70 \leq s < 80$	37		
$80 \leq s < 90$	8		
$90 \leq s < 100$	4		
Total	100		

(a) Copy the table and use it to calculate an estimate of the mean speed of these cars.

The speed limit is 70 miles per hour.

(b) Francis uses the information in the table to estimate the probability that the next car to pass is travelling at less than 70 miles per hour. What is this probability?

Probability ► page 88

MEG/ULEAC (SMP)

4 This graph summarises the amount collected in a day by 41 people collecting for charity.

(a) Estimate the total amount collected.

(b) Calculate an estimate of the mean amount that a person collects.

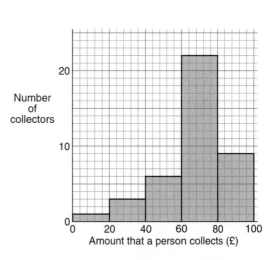

Answers and hints ► page 143

Cumulative frequency

This table shows the frequency of 27 items of data in 5-year intervals.

Age (years)	Frequency
$0 \leq x < 5$	4
$5 \leq x < 10$	7
$10 \leq x < 15$	10
$15 \leq x < 20$	4
$20 \leq x < 25$	2
Total	27

This shows the same data in a **cumulative frequency table.** This time it shows how many items have values less than the maximum for each interval.

Age (years)	Cumulative frequency
$0 \leq x < 5$	4
$0 \leq x < 10$	11
$0 \leq x < 15$	21
$0 \leq x < 20$	25
$0 \leq x < 25$	27

The data can be shown as points on a **cumulative frequency graph**. A curved line is drawn through the points.

The **median** is the value of the 'halfway' item, when they are placed in order of size – in this case it is the value of the 14th item. It can be estimated from the graph.

In a similar way you can estimate the value of the 'quarter-way' (the **first quartile**) and 'three-quarters-way' items (the **third quartile**).

The difference between these values is the **inter-quartile range**. It measures how 'spread out' the main part of the data is, ignoring the extremely high and low values.

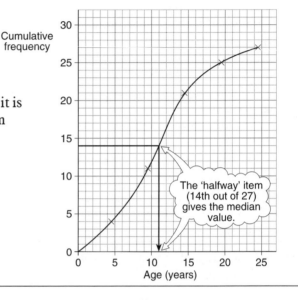

The 'halfway' item (14th out of 27) gives the median value.

1   Two weather stations in different countries have recorded the annual rainfall for 50 years. The cumulative frequency graph for Amber weather station is shown below.

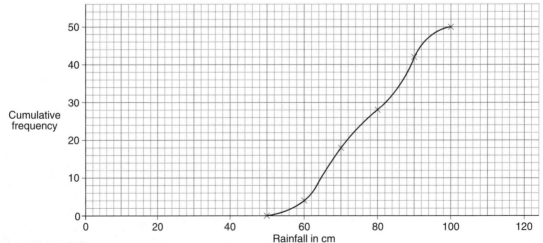

(a) From this graph, find:
   (i) the median annual rainfall at Amber   (ii) the inter-quartile range

The frequency distribution for these 50 years at Baron weather station is given in this table.

(b) Find the cumulative frequencies and draw the frequency graph for Baron.

(c) Compare the annual rainfall at Amber and Baron. You should make at least two comments.

MEG/ULEAC (SMP)

Annual rainfall (r cm)	Frequency
$30 < r \le 40$	2
$40 < r \le 50$	4
$50 < r \le 60$	5
$60 < r \le 70$	6
$70 < r \le 80$	10
$80 < r \le 90$	12
$90 < r \le 100$	5
$100 < r \le 110$	3
$110 < r \le 120$	3

2 The number of days' absence of 280 workers in a factory during one year was recorded. The results are in this frequency table.

(a) Copy the table and complete the cumulative frequency column.

(b) Draw the cumulative frequency graph.

(c) Use the graph to find the median number of days' absence.

(d) Approximately how many workers were absent for more than 18 days?

Number of days absent	Frequency	Cumulative frequency
0–5	32	32
6–10	67	99
11–15	131	
16–20	43	
21–30	7	

MEG/ULEAC (SMP)

3 The table below shows the weekly incomes (correct to the nearest pound) of 500 married couples over retirement age in 1992 in Camberton.

Income (£)	Number of couples	Cumulative frequency
0–50	17	
51–100	189	
101–150	215	
151–200	42	
201–600	37	

(a) Copy the table and complete the cumulative frequency column.

(b) Draw a cumulative frequency graph for the data.

(c) Use the graph to estimate the median income.

(d) Copy and complete this sentence:

'In 1992, 75% of retired couples in Camberton had incomes of £... or less per week.'

MEG (SMP)

Answers and hints ► page 144

Scatter diagrams

A scatter diagram is used to see whether there appears to be a relationship between two features, such as the handspan and height of the people in a particular group.

Each pair of values that relates to one member is plotted as a point.
Sometimes this gives a pattern where the points appear to lie clustered around a line – the 'line of best fit'. In such cases there is said to be **correlation** between the features.
Even where there is correlation, you cannot say that one set of values is **determined** by the other set.

Here are five examples drawn to the same scale.
They show different patterns of correlation.

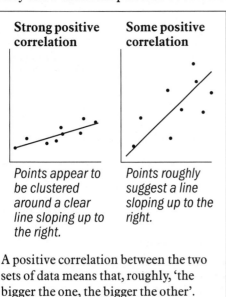

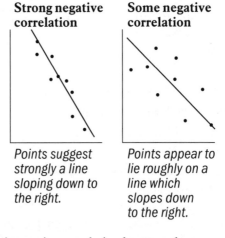

Strong positive correlation	**Some positive correlation**	**Strong negative correlation**	**Some negative correlation**	**No correlation**
Points appear to be clustered around a clear line sloping up to the right.	*Points roughly suggest a line sloping up to the right.*	*Points suggest strongly a line sloping down to the right.*	*Points appear to lie roughly on a line which slopes down to the right.*	*No obvious line emerges from looking at the points.*

A positive correlation between the two sets of data means that, roughly, 'the bigger the one, the bigger the other'.

A negative correlation between the two sets of data means that, roughly, 'the bigger the one, the smaller the other'.

1   In the southern hemisphere, the latitude of a place measures in degrees how far south of the equator it is.
The table below gives some information about the latitude and the temperature in degrees Celsius of eight Australian cities.

City	Latitude in degrees South	Annual mean maximum temperature (°C)
Adelaide	34·9	22·4
Brisbane	27·4	25·4
Canberra	35·3	19·3
Darwin	12·3	32·3
Hobart	42·8	16·7
Melbourne	37·7	19·7
Perth	32·0	23·1
Sydney	33·9	21·4

(a) Plot this information on a grid to make a scatter diagram.

(b) What conclusion can you make from your scatter diagram?

MEG/ULEAC (SMP)

2   The table gives the age in months to the nearest month and the height in metres
    to the nearest centimetre of 12 girls in a Year 10 class.

Age	182	182	183	184	184	185	186	186	187	188	189	190
Height	1·70	1·80	1·58	1·68	1·72	1·59	1·57	1·63	1·73	1·54	1·81	1·60

(a) Draw a scatter diagram for this set of data.

(b) Is there any relationship between the ages and the heights? Explain your answer.

The school has pupils aged from 11 to 16 years.
The heights of all the girls were measured.

(c) Describe the sort of relationship there is likely to be between
    their age in years and their height in centimetres.   MEG/ULEAC (SMP)

3   The table shows the names, capacities, lengths, surface areas and prices for some garden ponds.

Design	Capacity (l)	Length (cm)	Surface area (m²)	Cost (£)
Blackbird	365	196	1·4	90
Dove	475	137	1·2	100
Jay	180	155	0·7	50
Kestrel	635	180	2·0	120
Linnet	365	203	1·3	80
Swift	75	137	0·5	30
Thrush	705	282	2·3	120

These scatter diagrams show pairs of data for each pond.

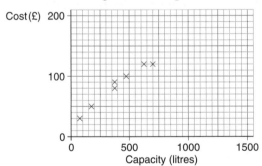

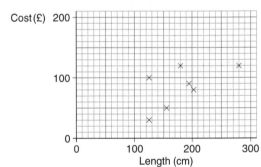

(a) What can you say about the capacity and the cost?

(b) What can you say about the length and the cost?

4   Mrs Bennett wants to buy a Carapace caravan.
    She looked in a magazine and saw these second-hand
    caravans for sale.

    (a) (i) Draw a scatter diagram for these data.
        (ii) Describe the relationship between age and price.

    (b) (i) Draw a line of best fit on your diagram.
        (ii) How much would Mrs Bennett expect to pay
             for a six-year-old Carapace caravan?

Age (years)	Price (£)
3	7500
5	6000
4	6000
4	7000
7	4195
5	5750
3	8000
2	8500
9	2500

Probability 1

The **probability** of something happening is a value telling you how likely it is to happen.
0 means it never happens. 1 (or 100%) means it always happens.
You can give a probability as a fraction, a decimal or a percentage.

If you assume that things like dice used in probability experiments are unbiased (fair),
you can work out probabilities without doing an experiment.

There are 4 white balls and 3 black balls in the bag.

So the probability of pulling out a white ball is $\frac{4}{7}$.

The number of balls with the colour you want

The total number of balls

If you have done an experiment a lot of times you can work out a probability from it.

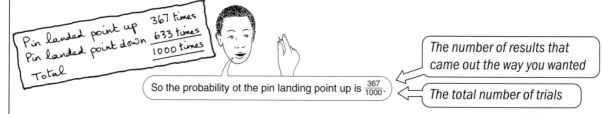

Pin landed point up   367 times
Pin landed point down   633 times
Total   1000 times

So the probability ot the pin landing point up is $\frac{367}{1000}$.

The number of results that came out the way you wanted

The total number of trials

The probability of something happening plus the probability of it not happening
always equals 1 (or 100%).

There's a 25% chance of rain.

So the probability of it not raining is 75%.

1   A normal 6-sided dice has dots representing
    the numbers 1, 2, 3, 4, 5 and 6 on its faces.
    The dice is thrown.

    Write down as a fraction the probability that the number at the top will be

    (a) 5,

    (b) less than 5.

                                                                              MEG

2   In Nicolette's pencil case there are 4 blue, 1 red, 3 black and 2 green pens.
    She takes a pen out without looking at it.
    What is the probability that it is

    (a) red,

    (b) black or blue?

                                                                    MEG/ULEAC (SMP)

3   An 8-sided dice is numbered   0, 0, 0, 1, 1, 1, 1, 2.

    (a) What is the probability of getting a 0 on one throw?

    (b) What is the probability of **not** getting a 2?

4 This diagram shows an unbiased lucky spinner game used at a school fete.
It consists of 8 equal sectors.
The pointer is spun once and, when it stops, shows how much money the player wins.

(spinner showing sectors: 2p, 5p, 0, 0, 5p, 20p, 10p, 0)

(a) What is the probability that a player wins 20p?

(b) What is the probability that a player wins no money?

MEG (SMP)

5 In a game of Bingo, the numbers 1 to 90 are drawn out of a bag one at a time.
This is David's card.   ⇨

(a) How many numbers are there on his card?

(b) What is the probability that the first number to be drawn is one of David's numbers?

3		21	32			63	70	
	15	24		46	54		76	
	19	28	37		58			89

MEG/ULEAC (SMP)

6 A Girl Guide group sells 400 raffle tickets to raise funds.
Kate sells 50 tickets to members of her family.
What is the probability that one of Kate's family will win first prize?
Give your answer as a fraction in its simplest form.

7 Ravi does an experiment dropping a paper cup a lot of times.
He works out some experimental probabilities.

The probability of it landing upside-down is 0·08.

The probability of it landing on its side is 0·89.

What is the probability of it landing the right way up?

8 Pierre throws a cricket bat into the air and makes a note of whether it lands on its front or on its back.
He does this 50 times. Here are his results.

(a) How many times did the cricket bat
  (i) land on its front,
  (ii) land on its back?

	Tally	Frequency
Landed on front	卌 卌 卌 卌 l	
Landed on back	卌 卌 卌 卌 卌 llll	

(b) Work out the experimental probability of
  (i) the cricket bat landing on its front,
  (ii) the cricket bat landing on its back.

(c) If you threw the bat in the air 100 times, about how many times would you expect it to land on its front?

MEG (SMP)

9 Laura spun a 10p coin many times.
She got 'heads' 612 times.
The number of times she spun the coin is one of these:

800   1200   1600   2000

Write which one it is likely to have been.
Explain why you chose this answer.

MEG (SMP)

Answers and hints ► page 146

All the possible ways

In some questions you have to make a list of all the different ways of **arranging** things, like showing all the ways of putting three counters – red, yellow and blue – in a line.

Arrange them with red in the first place.

Keep red first but change the order of the other two.

Check: are there any other arrangements with red in the first place?

Now put a different colour first and carry on the same way.

Red	Yellow	Blue
Red	Blue	Yellow
Yellow	Red	Blue

With the counters, if you put red in one place it couldn't go in another.

In some other questions, what goes in one place does not affect what goes in other places.

For example, if you throw a 1 to 4 dice and a 1 to 6 dice together, the result on one dice is not restricted by the result on the other.

You can show all the ways in a table like this.

Number on second dice

	1	2	3	4	5	6
1	1,1	1,2	1,3	1,4	1,5	1,6
2	2,1	2,2	2,3	2,4	2,5	2,6
3	3,1	3,2	3,3	3,4	3,5	3,6
4	4,1	4,2	4,3	4,4	4,5	4,6

Number on first dice

If you have to find the probability of a particular total score, it helps to put total scores in your table, rather than pairs of results.

The probability of getting a total of 2 is $\frac{1}{24}$ (1 possibility out of 24 equally likely ones).

The probability of getting a total of 5 or more is $\frac{18}{24}$ (18 possibilities out of 24 equally likely ones).

Number on second dice

	1	2	3	4	5	6
1	2	3	4	5	6	7
2	3	4	5	6	7	8
3	4	5	6	7	8	9
4	5	6	7	8	9	10

Number on first dice

1 Michael has these three cards. List all the different ways that he can arrange them. Start the list like this.

3	4	5
3	5	4

2 Mandy has three tee-shirts, a red one, a white one and a yellow one. She has two pairs of trousers, a grey pair and a blue pair. Continue this list of all the choices of tee-shirt and trousers she can wear.

MEG/ULEAC (SMP)

Choices

Tee-shirt	Trousers
Red	Blue

3

MENU

First course
Soup or Pate

Second course
Cannelloni or Lamb or Fish

Third course
Gateau or Trifle

List all the different three-course meals you could have from this menu.
(You can use abbreviations like S for soup, and so on.)

4 In a game you spin both of these arrows when it's your go.
You see what numbers the arrows point to.
You add them to get your total score.

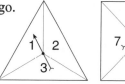

(a) Copy and complete this table showing the totals for
all the possible results.

(b) What is the probability of scoring a total of 9?

(c) What is the probability of scoring a total of 7 or less?

	4	5	6	7
1		6		
2				
3				

5  Tom's money box has a simple combination lock.
It has two dials.
The first dial has the numbers 2, 4, 6, 8 on it and
the second dial has the numbers 1, 3, 5, 7 on it.

The picture shows the combination 2 1.

(a) Use a table or diagram to show all the possible combinations.

(b) Tom has forgotten his combination.
He knows that the sum of the digits is eleven.
He tries one combination with digits adding up to eleven.
What is the probability that it will open the money box?

MEG (SMP)

6 Tim's cash card lets him obtain money from a cash machine at the bank.
The card has a four-figure code number.
Tim knows that the digits are 2, 3, 5, 8 and that
it starts with an odd digit and ends with an even digit.

(a) List all the possible code numbers that Tim might try.

(b) The machine allows three attempts at getting it right before
keeping the card. What is the probability that
Tim will be able to get some money from the machine?

MEG/ULEAC (SMP)

7 The white dice has faces marked 1, 2, 3, 3, 4, 5.
The black dice has faces marked 2, 3, 4, 4, 5, 6.

(a) Use a table or diagram to show all the equally likely outcomes
from throwing the two dice together.

(b) Trish calculates that the probability of a double 3 is $\frac{1}{36}$.
Is she right? Give a reason for your answer.

(c) What is the most likely total when you throw the two dice together?

8 Carol sells three flavours of ice lollies, orange, lemon
and chocolate.
Patrick wants to buy three lollies.
In a table list the ten different choices he could make.
The first one has been done.

Orange	Lemon	Chocolate
3	0	0

MEG/ULEAC (SMP)

Answers and hints ► page 147

Probability 2

If you are dealing with an experiment that has more than one stage or event, a tree diagram is a useful way to record the probabilities.

When the events are independent

Example

Calculate the probability of getting just one 6 when an ordinary fair dice is thrown twice.

The dice has no memory so the probabilities for the second throw are the same as for the first.

To get these probabilities multiply together the probabilities along the branches.

First throw → $\frac{1}{6}$ **Second throw** **Outcome**

	6 6, 6	$\frac{1}{36}$
$\frac{1}{6}$ 6	$\frac{5}{6}$ Not 6 6, Not 6	$\frac{5}{36}$
$\frac{5}{6}$ Not 6	$\frac{1}{6}$ 6 Not 6, 6	$\frac{5}{36}$
	$\frac{5}{6}$ Not 6 Not 6, Not 6	$\frac{25}{36}$

The probability of just one 6 is $\frac{5}{36} + \frac{5}{36} = \frac{10}{36}$.

When the result for one event affects the probabilities for another event

Example

A bag contains 3 red balls and 2 blue ones. A ball is taken out and not replaced. A second ball is taken out.

Calculate the probability of getting just one red.

There are now 2 red and 2 blue so the probabilities change.

First ball **Second ball** **Outcome**

$\frac{3}{5}$ R	$\frac{2}{4}$ R R, R	$\frac{6}{20}$
	$\frac{2}{4}$ B R, B	$\frac{6}{20}$
$\frac{2}{5}$ B	$\frac{3}{4}$ R B, R	$\frac{6}{20}$
	$\frac{1}{4}$ B B, B	$\frac{2}{20}$

The probability of just one red is $\frac{6}{20} + \frac{6}{20} = \frac{12}{20}$.

There are now 3 red and 1 blue so the probabilities change.

---

1 There are 3 cracked eggs and 9 perfect eggs in a box. Finbar chooses 2 eggs at random from this box.

(a) Copy and complete the tree diagram.

(b) Find the probability that Finbar chooses at least one cracked egg.

First egg **Second egg**

$\frac{3}{12}$ Cracked, $\frac{9}{11}$, Perfect, Cracked, Perfect, Cracked

MEG

2 A bag contains 3 red balls, 2 blue balls and 5 green balls. Two balls are drawn from the bag, one after the other, and not replaced.

(a) What is the probability that they are both blue?

(b) What is the probability that they are both the same colour?

MEG (SMP)

3 A sweet factory makes chocolate bars.
One day the chocolate does not harden properly and
$\frac{1}{6}$ of the bars are mis-shapen and have to be rejected.

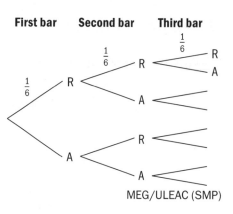

    (a) Three bars are selected at random and inspected.
Copy and complete this tree diagram to show the
probabilities of them being rejected (R) or accepted (A).

    (b) Calculate the probability of
       (i) these three bars being all accepted,
      (ii) having two of these three bars rejected and
          the other accepted.

MEG/ULEAC (SMP)

4 Anwar has to go through two sets of traffic lights as he cycles to school.

The probability that he has to stop at the first set of lights is 0·6.
If he has to stop at this set, the probability that he will then have
to stop at the second set is 0·3.
If he does not stop at the first set, the probability that he has to
stop at the second set is 0·8.

    (a) What is the probability that he will not have to stop at the first set of lights?

    (b) By drawing a tree diagram or otherwise, find
       (i) the probability that Anwar does not have to stop at
          any traffic lights on his way to school,
      (ii) the probability that he has to stop at just one set of traffic lights.

MEG/ULEAC (SMP)

5 A cricket team has three jobs that need doing at the end of each game.
Each job is allocated a coloured ball:

      Blue: pack the bag
      Red: write a match report
      Yellow: clean the changing room

As well as these 3 coloured balls there are also 8 white balls:

      White: no job today

At the end of the game each player in the team picks one of these balls out of a bag.

One Saturday, after four of the team had chosen, there were
7 balls left in the bag – the blue and the yellow and 5 white.
What is the probability that the next two players to choose will
each have a job to do?

MEG/ULEAC (SMP)

6 A box contains 10 cards of which 2 are red and 8 are black.
A card is picked at random, its colour is noted and then it is replaced.
This is done three times.

    (a) Draw a tree diagram to illustrate all the possible outcomes.

    (b) Calculate the probability that exactly two of the three cards picked are red.

Now three cards are picked at random, one after the other, and not replaced.

    (c) Calculate the probability that all three cards are black.

MEG (SMP)

Answers and hints ► page 148

Mixed handling data

1   This graph shows the number of TV licences sold in England and Wales.

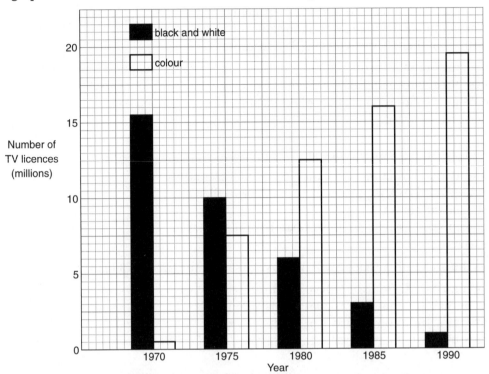

(a) How many black and white TV licences were sold in 1975?

(b) How many TV licences were sold altogether in 1985?

(c) In 1980 more colour TV licences than black and white TV licences were sold.
    How many more was this?

MEG (SMP)

2   This table shows some information about the pupils in a maths class.

	Dark hair	Fair hair
Girls	4	10
Boys	9	5

(a) How many pupils are in the class?

(b) How many girls are in the class?

(c) How many pupils have fair hair?

(d) What is the probability that a pupil chosen at random from the class
     (i) is a girl,
     (ii) has fair hair,
     (iii) is a boy with dark hair?

NICCEA

94

3 This graph shows Rhona's height from her first to her tenth birthday.

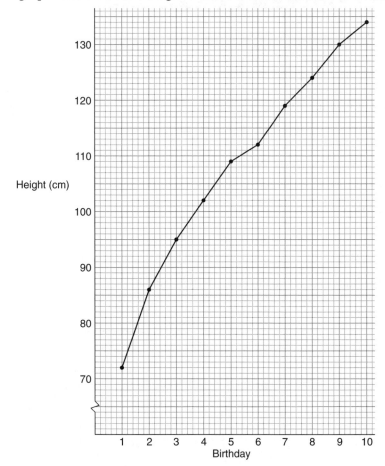

Use the graph to answer these questions.

(a) What was Rhona's height on her fifth birthday?

(b) How much did she grow in the next two years?

(c) How much did she grow between her first and tenth birthdays?

(d) (i) Between which two consecutive birthdays did she grow the most?
    (ii) How much was this?

MEG/ULEAC (SMP)

4 Fred thinks that the Conservatives will win the local by-election easily.
He telephoned some people on a Friday morning and asked them
how they intend to vote.
He obtained these results.

Conservative	17
Labour	8
Lib-Dem	5

Fred says this is clear evidence that the Conservatives will win.
Give, briefly, three reasons why this statement is not justified.

MEG (SMP)

Answers and hints ► page 151

MIXED AND ORALLY-GIVEN QUESTIONS

Mixed questions 1

1 This diagram represents a farmer's field.

(a) Work out the perimeter of the field.

The farmer decides to put up a new fence around the perimeter of the field.
It costs £1·50 to put up one metre of fence.

(b) How much would it cost to fence the whole field?

(c) Work out the area of the field.

The farmer wants to plant seed in the field.
Seed is sold in sacks.
Each sack contains 20 kg of seed.
One kilogram of seed covers 14 m².

(d) How many kilograms of seed does it take to cover the whole field?

(e) How many sacks does the farmer need to buy to plant this field with seed?

ULEAC

2 The diagram represents a measuring jug calibrated in millilitres, fluid ounces and pints.
Some of the numbers have worn off; they are indicated by letters.

(a) Write down the values of P, Q and R.

(b) How many fluid ounces are there in 8 pints?

(c) Using the diagram, estimate
   (i) the number of litres in $1\frac{1}{2}$ pints,
   (ii) the number of fluid ounces in $\frac{1}{4}$ litre.

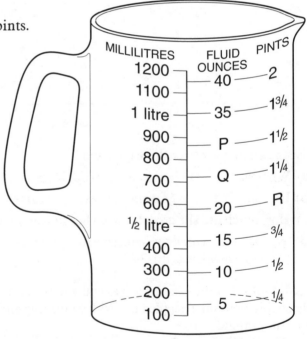

MEG

3 (a) One Christmas day the temperature in London fell to a low of ⁻5 °C at 02:00 and a high of 7 °C at 13:15.
   By how many degrees did the temperature change?

(b) On the same day the sun rose at 07:44 and set at 15:55.
   How much daylight was there?
   Give your answer in hours and minutes.

4 A caterpillar moves 267 centimetres in one hour.

(a) What is its average speed in metres per second?
Give your answer to 2 significant figures.

(b) Write your answer to (a) in standard index form.   MEG/ULEAC (SMP)

5 A metalworker has to replace an old drill bit of $\frac{3}{8}$ inch diameter.
The shop sells metric sizes only.
Given that 1 metre is approximately 39·37 inches, calculate,
in mm correct to the nearest 0·5 mm, the diameter of
the nearest equivalent metric drill bit.

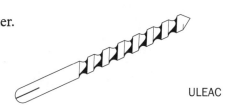

ULEAC

6 One angle of a triangle is 60°. For the other two angles the larger one is
five times the smaller.
Find what all the angles are.

7

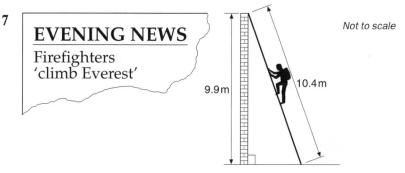

EVENING NEWS
Firefighters
'climb Everest'

9.9 m   10.4 m

Not to scale

To raise sponsor money for charity, some firefighters took turns
climbing a ladder to the top of a wall.

(a) Safety regulations state that the angle between the ladder and
the ground should be between 71° and 76°.

Calculate the angle between the ladder and the ground shown in
the diagram above, to confirm that this is within the safety limits.

(b) The firefighters climbed the ladder again and again, until between
them they had climbed a total vertical height equal to the height
of Mount Everest, 8848 m.
(i) How many times was the ladder climbed?
(ii) Each time the ladder was climbed, £5 was given to charity.
How much money was raised altogether for charity?   MEG

8 Shahida has a fish pond, in the shape of a circle of diameter 240 cm,
in which she wishes to keep some fish.
She has read that for every 1000 cm² of water surface
you can keep ten centimetres of fish.
This could be one 10 cm fish or two 5 cm fish and so on.

(a) Calculate the surface area of the water.

(b) If she knew that eventually the fish would grow to an average length
of 15 cm, how many fish at most should she put in the pond?   WJEC

Answers and hints ► page 152

Mixed questions 2

1

The weather map shows temperatures in degrees Celsius (°C),
and wind speeds in miles per hour (m.p.h.).
The arrows show the direction in which the wind is blowing.

(a) What is the highest temperature shown on the map?

(b) **From** which direction is the wind blowing at 10 m.p.h?

(c) The formula for changing degrees Celsius (°C) to degrees Fahrenheit (°F) is

$$F = \frac{9C}{5} + 32.$$

Use the formula to calculate the temperature in Belfast in degrees Fahrenheit.   MEG

2 During 1987/8 there were 23 million telephone directories printed.

(a) Write this number in standard form.

(b) One tonne is equal to 10^3 kg. The directories used 27 350 tonnes of paper.
Write this in kilograms in standard form.

(c) What was the mean average mass of paper in one directory?

(d) Explain how you know whether your answer to part (c) is sensible.   MEG/ULEAC (SMP)

3 A carton of milk is shaped so that its top is
   a circle of diameter 8·0 cm and its base is
   a square of side 6·4 cm.

   (a) Find the area of the top of the carton in cm².

   (b) Find the area of the base of the carton in cm².

   (c) When full, the carton contains 1 litre of milk.
       Assume that the volume can be calculated by the formula

       $$\text{volume} = \frac{\text{area of top} + \text{area of base}}{2} \times \text{height}.$$

       Find the height of the carton.

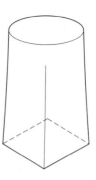

MEG/ULEAC (SMP)

4 All of the following calculations are wrong.
   Show clearly, **without calculating the exact answer**, how you can tell
   that they are wrong.

   (a) The circumference of a circle of radius 5 metres is calculated as 15·7 metres.

   (b) $\dfrac{4\cdot73}{0\cdot98 \times 0\cdot89} = 4\cdot68$

   (c) $(1\cdot8 \times 10^4)^2 \times 1\cdot7 = 8\cdot508 \times 10^8$

MEG (SMP)

5 250 squash balls were tested by dropping them from 2 metres.
   Their rebound heights are given in the following table.

Height (h) in cm	Frequency
$15 \leq h \leq 25$	30
$25 < h \leq 35$	35
$35 < h \leq 45$	48
$45 < h \leq 55$	58
$55 < h \leq 65$	60
$65 < h \leq 75$	19

   (a) Draw a cumulative frequency graph of this information

   (b) The balls are rejected if they bounce to less than 50 cm.
       What percentage of this sample is rejected?

   (c) What is the median height of bounce of this sample?

   (d) Compare your answers to (b) and (c). Do you think that
       the batch of balls from which this sample was taken is any good?
       Give a reason for your answer.

6 The angles of a triangle ABC are x, x and $(x - 30°)$.

   (a) What sort of triangle is ABC?

   (b) Write down an equation in x.

   (c) Solve your equation and calculate the size of angle B.

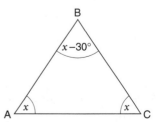

MEG

Answers and hints ► page 152

Mixed questions 3

1 The odd numbers 1, 3, 5, 7, 9, ... are written in a triangular block as follows:

1st row	1			
2nd row	3	5		
3rd row	7	9	11	
4th row	13	15	17	19
5th row	21	—	—	—	—

(a) Write down the five numbers which will appear in the 5th row.

(b) For the 7th row, write down
   (i) the first number,
   (ii) the last number.

(c) Copy and complete the following table to show the total and the mean (average) of the numbers in each row.

Row	1	2	3	4	5	6
Total	1					
Mean	1					

(d) For the nth row of the triangular block, write down (in terms of n)
   (i) the total of the numbers,   (ii) the mean of the numbers.

MEG

2

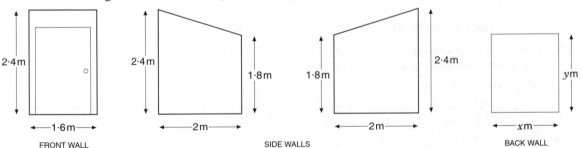

This is a sketch of a simple shed.
Simon is going to cover the outside of all the walls (and the door) with a waterproof sealant.

These are drawings of the four walls (not to scale).

2·4m   1·6m   FRONT WALL

2·4m   1·8m   2m   SIDE WALLS

1·8m   2·4m   2m   SIDE WALLS

2·4m ym xm   BACK WALL

The floor is a rectangle.

(a) Work out the area of the front wall (including the door).

(b) (i) What is the width of the back wall (x)?
   (ii) What is the height of the back wall (y)?
   (iii) Work out the area of the back wall.

MEG/ULEAC (SMP)

3 Counters numbered 2 to 9 are put in a bag.

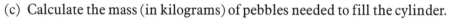

(a) Which of the numbers 2 to 9 are multiples of 3?

(b) Which of the numbers 2 to 9 have both 2 and 3 as factors?

(c) One of the counters is drawn at random.
What is the probability that it has both 2 and 3 as factors?

WJEC

4 (a) Joanna travels a distance of 75 miles at an average speed
of 30 miles per hour. How long does the journey take?

(b) Write down an expression for the time taken to travel
a distance of x miles at a speed of s miles per hour.

NICCEA

5 A sewage treatment works is being built. The untreated water is to
drain through pebbles in a container.
The container is in the shape of a cylinder with diameter 8 m.
The cylinder is 2 m high.

(a) Calculate the area (in square metres) of the top of the cylinder.

(b) Calculate the volume (in cubic metres) of the cylinder.

On average the mass of the pebbles is 800 kg per m^3.

(c) Calculate the mass (in kilograms) of pebbles needed to fill the cylinder.

The pebbles were brought to the sewage treatment works in lorries.
Each lorry carried 20 tonnes.

(d) How many lorry loads were needed to fill the cylinder?

ULEAC

6 From 1995 spirits have been sold in measures of 25 ml.
Before that, in England, the measure was $\frac{1}{6}$ gill.

> 4 gills = 1 pint
> 1 pint = 568 ml

(a) How many millimetres is $\frac{1}{6}$ gill?

(b) What is the percentage increase in a measure?

MEG/ULEAC (SMP)

7 Rutland Water is a man-made lake.
Its capacity is 124 000 million litres, to the nearest 1000 million litres.

(a) What is the smallest value for the capacity?

The surface area of the lake is 1255 hectares.
1 hectare = 10 000 m^2, 1 m^3 = 1000 litres.

(b) Calculate the average depth of the lake in metres.

MEG/ULEAC (SMP)

8 The diagram shows a square tile in which
the pattern is symmetrical about both diagonals.
Find the area of the **unshaded** part of the tile in terms of x.

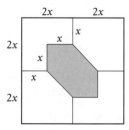

NICCEA

Answers and hints ► page 153

Orally-given questions 1

Some GCSE examinations have a short test where the questions are read out to you.
Practise by asking someone to read these questions to you.
He or she should read each question twice and then allow the appropriate amount of time.

Do not do any working for these questions.
You will be allowed ten seconds to answer each one.

1 What is the square root of eighty-one?

2 Write the fraction two-fifths as a percentage.

3 Draw a line (without using a ruler) which is about four centimetres long.

4 What length of fencing will be needed to fence in a square field of side sixty metres?

5 Write down a two-digit prime number that ends in a seven.

6 What is the difference between one hundred and fifty-six and ninety-eight?

You may use a pencil and paper for working out these questions.
You will be allowed thirty seconds to answer each one.

7 A fifty pence coin weighs thirteen point five grams. What would two weigh?

8 If *a* is four, what is *a* minus six?

9 An African lion can weigh as much as four hundred pounds.
   About how many kilograms is this?

10 In a sale all goods were reduced by twenty-five per cent.
   Liza bought a pair of shoes which would have cost twenty pounds before the sale.
   How much money did she save by buying them in the sale?

11 A sack of cement weighs one hundred and twelve pounds.
   How many pounds will forty-one of these sacks weigh?

12 Write down a rough answer to seventy-two point two multiplied by
   fifty-eight point nine.

13 Write the fraction thirty-four over fifty as a decimal.

14 Solve the equation four *x* add one equals twenty-one.

15 The distance round a circular pond is sixty-six metres.
   What is its diameter roughly?

16 Divide two point one by one hundred.

17 What is the volume in cubic centimetres of a small box measuring
   three centimetres by four centimetres by point five centimetres?

18 Sketch as accurately as you can an angle of one hundred and thirty degrees.

Answers and hints ► page 154

Orally-given questions 2

You are not allowed to do any working for these questions.
You will be allowed ten seconds to answer each one.

1   Write in figures three hundred and twenty-six thousand and eighty-five.

2   What is the area in square centimetres of a rectangle six centimetres by nine centimetres?

3   Cheap electric kettles cost five pounds each.
    How much would it cost to buy three hundred of them at this price?

4   Write down the reciprocal of two.

5   A swimming pool is twenty metres long.
    How many lengths do I need to swim to cover six hundred metres?

6   Two interior angles of a triangle add up to one hundred and sixty degrees.
    What is the size of the third interior angle?

7   What is the sum of fifteen, twenty and thirty-five?

You may use a pencil and paper for working out these questions.
You will be allowed thirty seconds to answer each one.

8   What is the value of four cubed?

9   The population of the United Kingdom is about fifty-five million.
    Doctors think that up to twenty per cent of the population suffer from
    some form of eczema. How many people is this?

10 Isha needs one hundred and six carpet tiles for her new flat.
    They come in boxes of twenty tiles. How many boxes will she need to buy?

11 I think of a number. I multiply it by ten and add three.
    The answer is ninety-three. What number did I think of?

12 What number lies exactly halfway between negative two and negative three?

13 The world record for tap dancing is held by Roy Castle.
    He managed one thousand four hundred and forty taps a minute.
    How many was this a second?

14 One litre is approximately zero point two of a gallon.
    Approximately how many gallons is eighty litres?

15 The temperature fell from three degrees Celsius to minus two degrees Celsius.
    What was the drop in temperature?

16 Add together five point six and one point seven.

17 Sketch the graph of y equals x squared for negative and positive values of x.

18 Afternoon school starts at one thirty p.m. and lasts one and three-quarter hours.
    At what time does afternoon school finish?

Answers and hints ► page 154

ANSWERS AND HINTS

Accuracy of answers

The accuracy of your answers is important. You will often have to decide for yourself on a suitable degree of accuracy; if you do not, you could lose a mark. In general, you should never give an answer to more accuracy than the data in the question and sometimes one figure less might be appropriate.

In multi-stage calculations you may need to give a rounded answer to one part of a question. If you use this answer in another part, be sure to use the unrounded answer in your calculation.

NUMBER

Properties of numbers (page 2)

1   (a) 18 $(6 \times 3 = 18)$

(b) 16 or 25

(c) 2 $(2 \times 2 \times 2 = 8)$

2   (a) 1, 2, 3, 4, 6, 8, 12, 24

(b) 31, 37, 41, 43, 47

(c) 8, 27, 64 $(2^3 = 8, 3^3 = 27, 4^3 = 64)$

3   $3^2 = 9$, $8^2 = 64$, $2^3 = 8$, $3^3 = 27$ and
$5^2 = 25$,   so the order is
2^3 3^2 5^2 3^3 8^2

4   $60 = 2 \times 2 \times 3 \times 5 = 2^2 \times 3 \times 5$
It is usual to write down the factors in numerical order.

5   (a) 2 is a factor of 4 and the three other numbers
are prime, so the smallest number
which is a multiple of 2, 3, 4 and 7
is $3 \times 4 \times 7 = 84$.

(b) Three possibilities are
64   $(8^2 = 64$ and $4^3 = 64)$
729   $(27^2$ and $9^3)$ and
1 000 000 $(1000^2$ and $100^3)$
You might have found another.

6   *Here are the methods for calculating the answers.*
You could have used a calculator.

(a) $\frac{1}{8} = 0 \cdot 125$ *Either answer is acceptable.*

(b) *First express the decimal as a fraction.*
$0 \cdot 04 = \frac{4}{100}$
The reciprocal of $\frac{4}{100}$ is $\frac{100}{4} = 25$.

(c) $0 \cdot 0005 = \frac{5}{10\,000} = \frac{1}{2000}$
The reciprocal is 2000.

(d) 5

(e) $\frac{9}{4} = 2 \cdot 25 = 2\frac{1}{4}$
Any of these answers is acceptable.

7   $168 = 4 \times 42 = 2 \times 2 \times 6 \times 7 = 2 \times 2 \times 2 \times 3 \times 7$
By looking at the factors of 168, you can find
the unknown number, 56.

8   (a) 23 or 29 or 31 or 37
You need give only one answer.

(b) 35

(c) 27 $(3 \times 3 \times 3 = 27)$

9   (a) The quilt is square so the length of a side
is given by $\sqrt{289}$ cm $= 17$ cm.

(b) $9^3 = 729$ and $10^3 = 1000$, so the largest cube
Sheena could make is one of side 9 units.

10 (a) The only square number less than 100
which is a multiple of 12 is 36.

(b) $56 = 2 \times 28 = 2 \times 2 \times 2 \times 7$.
Helen is thinking of 7.

More help or practice
Squares and square roots ► Book R1 page 38
Reciprocals ► Book R+ pages 26 to 27

Rounding (page 4)

1   (a) 6900   (b) 1100   (c) 26 200   (d) 1000
In (d), 9 is rounded up to 10.

2   $0 \cdot 10$ $0 \cdot 253$ $0 \cdot 3$ 1 $1 \cdot 03$

3 (a) 0·6   (b) 3·01   (c) 16·490

In (c), ·48971 is rounded up to ·490; the zero is the third decimal place.

4 10 million or 10 000 000

No marks would be given for '10'.

5 £18·75 × 25 = £468·75
$$= £469 \text{ (to the nearest pound)}$$

6 £145·5 ÷ 37·5 = £3·88

Notice that you need only key in 145·5 and not 145·50.

7 (a) 11 × 60 × 24 = 15 840 strikes per day

   (b) 15 840 × 365 = 5 781 600
$$= 6 \text{ million (to the nearest million)}$$

Remember that there are 60 minutes in 1 hour, 24 hours in 1 day and 365 days in 1 year.
Always ignore leap years in questions like this.

8 (a) £10·79 ÷ 2·5 = £4·316
$$= £4·32 \text{ to the nearest penny}$$
The first 2 decimal places in the answer represent pence – the '1' is rounded up to 2.

   (b) 2·5 × 14 m² = 35 m²

9 (a) 600 × 1·544 = 926·4
     Sally gets $926 to the nearest dollar.

   (b) 200 ÷ 2·384 = 83·89
     Tim gets £84 (to the nearest pound).

10 (a) *Start by converting £18 to pence so you are working with the same units.*
     Amount of petrol bought in litres
     = 1800 ÷ 47·8 = 37·657
     Cost of 37·657 litres at second garage
     = 37·657 × 51·3p = 1931·80p
     = £19·32 (to the nearest penny)
     Extra that would have been paid
     = £19·32 − £18·00
     = £1·32 (to the nearest penny)

    (b) Number of gallons = 37·657 ÷ 4·54
$$= 8·29 \text{ (to 2 d.p.)}$$

Remember not to round in the middle of a calculation. For example, if you round 37·657 litres to 38 litres before multiplying by 51·3 you would get the answer £19·49 instead of £19·32.

More help or practice

Round to nearest whole number ► Book B1 pages 15 to 18
Round to given number of decimal places
► Book B1 pages 26 to 32
Round to nearest penny ► Book B1 page 42
Decimal calculations with money ► Book B1 pages 41 to 42
Foreign exchange► Book R3 page 118

Significant figures (page 6)

1 (a) 49 000   (b) 0·03   (c) 59
   (d) 1010   (e) 0·000 71   (f) 0·9
   (g) 490   (h) 2·1   (i) 0·050

If you got some wrong these notes might help.

(b) Neither zero in 0·0348 is significant.

(e) The first significant figure is the '7'.

(g) The zero in the rounded 490 is significant.

(i) The right-hand zero is significant.

2 2 significant figures

3 155 m weighs 155 × 1·74 kg = 269·7 kg
$$= 270 \text{ kg (to 3 s.f.)}$$

4 35 litres = 35 ÷ 4·55 gallons
$$= 7·69 \text{ gallons}$$
$$= 7·7 \text{ gallons (to 2 s.f.)}$$

5 The thickness of one sheet = (2·6 ÷ 250) cm
$$= 0·0104 \text{ cm}$$
$$= 0·010 \text{ cm (to 2 s.f.)}$$

Note that an answer of '0·01' is correct only to 1 s.f.

More help or practice

Round to a given number of significant figures
► Book R1 pages 13 to 15

Negative numbers (page 7)

1 $^-5$ $^-3$ $^-1$ 0 2 3 4

2   (a) $^-13$ (b) 11 (c) 20 (d) $^-2\frac{1}{2}$ or $^-2 \cdot 5$ or $\frac{^-5}{2}$
    (e) 2 (f) $^-6$ (g) $^-1$ (h) $^-4$

3   (a) $(^-3 + 7)\,^\circ\text{C} = 4\,^\circ\text{C}$
    (b) $(^-3 - 7)\,^\circ\text{C} = ^-10\,^\circ\text{C}$

4   (a) $(17 - ^-13)\,^\circ\text{C} = 30\,^\circ\text{C}$
    (b) $(12 - ^-13)\,^\circ\text{C} = 25\,^\circ\text{C}$
       Maximum safe height $= 25 \times 100\,\text{m}$
                    $= 2500\,\text{m}$

5 $(20\,270 - ^-280)\,\text{ft} = 20\,550\,\text{ft}$
    $280\,\text{ft}$ below sea level is a negative elevation, of $^-280\,\text{ft}$.

> **More help or practice**
> Add and subtract negative numbers ► Book B1 pages 83 to 93,
> Book B+ pages 56 to 59
> Multiply and divide negative numbers ► Book B+ pages 60 to 61

Fractions (page 8)

1   (a) $\frac{3}{8} + \frac{3}{4} = \frac{3}{8} + \frac{6}{8} = \frac{9}{8} = 1\frac{1}{8}$

    (b) $\frac{2}{5} - \frac{1}{4} = \frac{8}{20} - \frac{5}{20} = \frac{3}{20}$

    (c) $1\frac{7}{8} - \frac{3}{4} = 1 + (\frac{7}{8} - \frac{6}{8}) = 1\frac{1}{8}$

    (d) $\frac{1}{2} + \frac{2}{3} + \frac{3}{4} = \frac{6}{12} + \frac{8}{12} + \frac{9}{12} = \frac{23}{12} = 1\frac{11}{12}$

    (e) $\frac{3}{4} \times \frac{1}{2} = \frac{3}{8}$

    (f) $\frac{7}{8} \div 2 = \frac{7}{8} \times \frac{1}{2} = \frac{7}{16}$

    (g) $\frac{5}{6} \times \frac{2}{3} = \frac{10}{18} = \frac{5}{9}$

    (h) $\frac{2}{5} \div \frac{1}{3} = \frac{2}{5} \times 3 = \frac{6}{5} = 1\frac{1}{5}$

2   (a) £8   (b) 20 cm   (c) 9 inches

3 $\frac{1}{4}$ of $50 = \frac{1}{4} \times 50 = \frac{25}{2} = 12\frac{1}{2}$

    $\frac{3}{8}$ of $24 = \frac{3}{8} \times 24^3 = 9$

    $\frac{1}{4}$ of £50 is the greater amount.

4   (a) Ash, $1\frac{3}{8}$ inches; oak, $1\frac{7}{8}$ inches

    (b) $1\frac{3}{8} + 1\frac{7}{8} = 3\frac{1}{4}$ inches, so Megan needs an

       extra $\frac{1}{4}$ inch of wood.

5   (a) $\frac{45}{120} = \frac{3}{8}$
       *Divide the top and bottom numbers by 15, the
       highest common factor, to write the fraction in its
       simplest form.*

    (b) $\frac{2}{3}$ of $45 = \frac{2}{3} \times 45 = 30$ bars

6   Total height in inches $= 6\frac{3}{4} + 1\frac{5}{8}$

                    $= 7 + \frac{3}{4} + \frac{5}{8}$

                    $= 7 + \frac{6}{8} + \frac{5}{8}$

                    $= 7 + \frac{6+5}{8} = 7 + \frac{11}{8}$

                    $= 7 + 1\frac{3}{8} = 8\frac{3}{8}$

7   (a) $\frac{2}{3}$ of £1·89 $= £1·89 \times \frac{2}{3}$
                $= £1·26$
    (b) $\frac{4}{3}$ of $250\,\text{ml} = \frac{1000}{3}\,\text{ml}$
                $= 333\frac{1}{3}\,\text{ml}$

> **More help or practice**
> Add and subtract fractions ► Book R+ page 52
> Multiply and simplify fractions ► Book R+ page 60

Fractions, decimals and percentages (page 10)

1 (a) 0.16 (b) 0.75 (c) 0.001 (d) 0.0625

2 (a) 81% (b) 37.5% (c) 72.5% (d) 68%

3 (a) $\frac{45}{100} = \frac{9}{20}$ (b) $\frac{9}{10}$

  (c) $\frac{66}{100} = \frac{33}{50}$ (d) $\frac{34}{100} = \frac{17}{50}$

4 (a) $16\,\text{kg}$ (b) £0.50 or 50p

  (c) £0.30 or 30p (d) $15\,\text{m}$

5 *Change each fraction to a decimal.*
  These decimals are correct to 2 decimal places.
  $\frac{7}{8} = 0.88,\ \frac{3}{5} = 0.60,\ \frac{5}{6} = 0.83,\ \frac{2}{3} = 0.67,\ \frac{5}{7} = 0.71,$
  so the order is $\frac{3}{5},\ \frac{2}{3},\ \frac{5}{7},\ \frac{5}{6},\ \frac{7}{8}.$

6 (a) 48 boys $(\frac{3}{5} \times 80)$ (b) 70% $(\frac{56}{80} \times 100)$

7 (a) 25% (b) 12% (c) 1.5% (d) 12.5%
  In (d) remember to use the same units when forming
  your fraction: £2 = 200p so $\frac{25}{200} = \frac{12.5}{100}$

8 $\frac{\text{Discount}}{\text{Original price}} \times 100\% = \frac{24}{150} \times 100\% = 16\%$

9 (a) 60% of the electorate voted.

  (b) $\frac{1}{4} \times \frac{3}{5} \times 100\% = 15\%$ voted for the Green Party.

  (c) $(100 - 15)\% = 85\%$ did not vote for the Green
     Party.

  In parts (b) and (c) the percentage is of the whole
  electorate, including people who did not choose to vote
  at all.

10 (a)

	streaky	middle	back	TOTAL
smoked	15	24	95	134
unsmoked	45	126	195	366
TOTAL	60	150	290	500

  (b) $\frac{134}{500} = \frac{268}{1000}$, so 26.8% of people preferred
     smoked bacon.
     The arithmetic here is easy enough to do in your
     head but you could have used a calculator.

11 (a) 28% of $46\,000 = 12\,880$ children

  (b) (i) $\frac{16\,100}{46\,000}$ is equivalent to 35%.

    (ii) $28\% + 35\% = 63\%$ are women or
       children.
       So $100\% - 63\% = 37\%$ are men.

12 (a) The reduction is £48\,000 − £42\,000 = £6000
     $\frac{6000}{48\,000}$ is equivalent to 12.5%.

  (b) £42\,000 × $\frac{1.5}{100}$ = £630

> **More help or practice**
> The equivalence of fractions, decimals and percentages
> ► Book B2 pages 88 to 94
> Fractions and percentages of a quantity
> ► Book RB+ pages 32 to 34

Percentages (page 12)

If you use the % key on your calculator, make sure you show
enough working to gain method marks in case you make a
mistake in keying.

1 VAT = £190 × $\frac{17.5}{100}$
   = £33.25

2 (a) £24.50 × 0.80 = £19.60

  (b) Old price × 0.80 = £42
     Old price   = £42 ÷ 0.8
            = £52.50

3 Population = 3000 × 1.1 × 1.1
        = 3630

4 Number of pupils last year = 988 ÷ 1.04
              = 950
   Check your answer by working out 950 × 1.04.

5 $\frac{755\,000}{680\,000} = 1.11 = 111\%$
   Percentage increase = $(111 - 100)\% = 11\%$
   You could have worked out the increase first
   (755\,000 − 680\,000 = 75\,000) and then found what
   percentage of 680\,000 this is.

6 (a) Mr Lee paid tax on £6400 − £2425 = £3975

(b) His income tax = 25% of £3975 = £993·75

(c) Mr Lee's national insurance contribution
= 7% of £6400 = £448

(d) His total deductions = £993·75 + £448
= £1441·75

(e) His net annual income = £6400 − £1441·75
= £4958·25

His net monthly income
= £413·19 (to the nearest penny)

7 The multipliers are 1·15 and 1·20.

$1·15 \times 1·20 = 1·38$

So the overall increase is 38%.

8 (a) Ian will pay £460 × 0·85 = £391.

(b) Lisa has a 35% discount. This means that

Full premium × 0·65 = £163·80

Full premium = £163·80 ÷ 0·65
= £252·00

More help or practice

Percentage increases and decreases ► Book R1 pages 81 to 83,
Book RB+ pages 37 to 39

Finding a percentage increase or decrease
► Book R1 pages 124 to 129

Income tax (with out-of-date figures!) ► Book R3 pages 16 to 17

VAT ► Book R3 pages 38 to 39

Insurance ► Book R3 pages 82 to 83

Saving ► Book R3 pages 88 to 90

Borrowing ► Book R3 pages 108 to 109

Compound percentages ► Book Y3 pages 92 to 96

Percentages backwards ► Book RB+ page 38

Ratio and proportion (page 14)

1 (a) 1 : 3   (b) 4 : 1   (c) 2 : 3

(d) 5 : 12   (e) 5 : 6   (f) 7 : 10

(g) 15 : 100 = 3 : 20   (h) 60 : 5 = 12 : 1

*Did you remember to change £1 to pence in (g) and
1 hour to minutes in (h), so that you had the same
units?*
Ratios in simplest form must not include fractions.

2 (a) *Divide £120 000 into 5 + 3 = 8 equal parts.*
$\frac{1}{8}$ *of £120 000 = £15 000*
Mrs Hanif invested £15 000 × 3 = £45 000

(b)   5 $\xrightarrow{\times 0·6}$ 3   The multiplier is 0·6.
£14 500   £?
So Mrs Hanif's share is £14 500 × 0·6 = £8700.
The total profit = £14 500 + £8700
= £23 200

*In this answer the multiplier method is used, but
the unitary method or any other would be equally
acceptable.*

3 12 cm weigh 8 grams

1 cm weighs $\frac{8}{12}$ grams

18 cm weigh $\frac{\overset{4}{8}}{\underset{2}{12}} \times \overset{3}{18}$ grams = 12 grams

*This is the unitary method, but the multiplier method
would be equally acceptable.*

4 (a) 27 g   (b) 200 g

5 Total frontage in metres = 27 + 34·5 + 18·5 = 80
$\frac{1}{80}$ of £5600 = £70
The largest payment = £70 × 34·5
= £2415

6 (a) 750 ml of vinegar

(b) Volume of oil in 1 litre (1000 ml)

$= \frac{5}{7} \times 1000 \, ml$

$= 714 \cdot 28 \, ml$

$= 710 \, ml$ (to the nearest 10 ml)

Volume of vinegar in 1 litre

$= \frac{2}{7} \times 1000 \, ml$

$= 285 \cdot 71 \, ml$

$= 290 \, ml$ (to the nearest 10 ml)

Having calculated one volume you could have subtracted it from 1000 to find the second volume. However, doing both calculations provides you with a check (710 + 290 = 1000).

7 The mixture ratio is 0·2 to 4·8 = 1 to 24.

More help or practice

Ratios (including simplest form) and sharing
► Book RB+ pages 53 to 60

The unitary method for proportion ► Book R3 pages 31 to 32

The multiplier method for proportion
► Book R2 pages 34 to 38, Book R3 pages 32 to 33

Estimation, checking and accuracy
(page 16)

1 $\frac{4780}{275} \approx \frac{4800}{300} = 16$ *by rounding the numbers to the nearest hundred.*

Other approximations would also be acceptable, for example $\frac{4780}{275} \approx \frac{5000}{250} = 20$.

You could also use multiplication to check:
$275 \times 17 \cdot 38 \approx 300 \times 20 = 6000$

2 The actual cost is £3·78 × 19.
A suitable estimate is £4 × 20 = £80.

3 $(860 \times 0 \cdot 28) \div (89 \div 3 \cdot 13)$
$\approx (900 \times 0 \cdot 3) \div (90 \div 3)$
$= 270 \div 30$
$= 9$

4 (a) 4·5   (b) 68·39   (c) 15·5
Rounded to 1 s.f. the calculations are:
(a) $\frac{50-30}{5} = \frac{20}{5} = 4$
(b) $7 \times (10 - 0 \cdot 07) \approx 70$
(c) $\frac{3}{0 \cdot 04 \times 5} = \frac{3}{0 \cdot 2} = 15$

5 (a) ⁻4·3   (b) 154·5   (c) 4·6
Suitable rough calculations are:
(a) $9 - (4 \times 3) = {}^-3$ (b) $\frac{90}{0 \cdot 5} = 180$
(c) $\frac{9-1}{3} \approx 3$

6 (a) 452 km (to the nearest km)
(b) £0·47 (to the nearest penny)
(c) £142·49 (to the nearest penny)

7 (a)
```
        25·58
   17) 435
       34
       95
       85
      100
       85
      150
      136
       14
```
$435 \div 17 = 25 \cdot 6$ (to 1 d.p.)
You may have used another quite acceptable method of doing this division.

(b) One possibility is to round to the nearest ten: $440 \div 20 = 22$; another is to use the inverse operation, multiplication, and round: $25 \cdot 6 \times 17 \approx 30 \times 17 = 510 \approx 435$.

8 (a) Acceptable estimates are 600, 640 or 650 miles and 70 or 75 litres.

   (b) One possible estimate for the number of miles per litre is $600 \div 70 \approx 9$.

9 (a) (2) is the only answer that could be correct.

   (b) In (1) the answer must end in 3 because $9 \times 7 = 63$.
   In (3), dividing by a number less than one increases the size of the answer.

More help or practice

Using a calculator ► Book R2 pages 1 to 4

Multiplication by a number less than 1
► Book B1 pages 43 to 45

Division by a number less than 1 ► Book B2 pages 18 to 20

Rough answers ► Book B1 pages 46 to 48,
Book R1 pages 17 to 18

Appropriate degree of accuracy ► Book R+ page 33

Indices (page 18)

1 (a) $810\,000$ (b) $0 \cdot 00065$ (c) $700\,000\,000$

2 (a) $4 \cdot 17 \times 10^5$ (b) $2 \cdot 17 \times 10^7$
   (c) $3 \cdot 04 \times 10^3$ (d) 6×10^7

3 (a) 6^5 (b) 2^5 (c) 10^6
   (d) $(10^2)^3 = 10^2 \times 10^2 \times 10^2 = 10^6$ (e) 10^2
   (f) $9 \div 3^4 = 3^2 \div 3^4 = 3^{-2}$
   (g) $2^3 \div 2^0 = 2^3 \div 1 = 2^3$
   (h) $5^4 \times 5 = 5^4 \times 5^1 = 5^5$ (i) a^4

4 (a) 1024 (b) $15\,625$
   (c) $0 \cdot 00243$ (d) 1024
   Notice the relation between (a) and (d).

5 (a) 7×10^3

   (b) If you write the numbers to 1 s.f. you get
   $(4 \times 10^7) \times (4 \times 10^{17}) = 16 \times 10^{24}$
   $= 1 \cdot 6 \times 10^{25}$
   The calculation is wrong by a factor of 10.

6 $(280 - 66)$ million $= 214$ million $= 2 \cdot 14 \times 10^8$
   Dinosaurs existed for $2 \cdot 14 \times 10^8$ years.

7 (a) (i) $9 \cdot 3 \times 10^7$ (ii) $1 \cdot 4 \times 10^{-4}$

   (b) (i) $(6 \cdot 7 \times 10^{-5}) \times (8 \cdot 3 \times 10^{12}) = 6 \cdot 7 \times 8 \cdot 3 \times 10^7$
   $= 55 \cdot 61 \times 10^7$
   $= 5 \cdot 561 \times 10^8$
   (ii) $\dfrac{3 \cdot 4 \times 10^2}{8 \cdot 84 \times 10^3} = 0 \cdot 384615 \times 10^{-5}$
   $= 3 \cdot 846\,15 \times 10^{-6}$

8 There are 24 hours in a day and 365 days in a year, so the total income is given by:
   $\$225\,000 \times 24 \times 365 = \$1 \cdot 971 \times 10^9$
   $= \$2 \cdot 0 \times 10^9$ (to 2 s.f.)

9 $8 \cdot 7^5 = 49\,842$ (to 5 s.f.)
   At this stage you must keep one more significant figure than you need in the answer.
   $8 \cdot 7 \times 10^5 = 870\,000$
   $870\,000 - 49\,842 = 820\,158 = 820\,200$ (to 4 s.f.) or
   $8 \cdot 202 \times 10^5$ (to 4 s.f.)
   Did you remember to use the power key $\boxed{\wedge}$ on your calculator to work out $8 \cdot 7^5$?

10 (a) 1 terawatt $= 1 \times 10^{12}$ watts
    51 terawatts $= 5 \cdot 1 \times 10^{13}$ watts

    (b) $6 \cdot 5 \times 10^2$ terawatts $= 6 \cdot 5 \times 10^2 \times 10^{12}$ watts
    $= 6 \cdot 5 \times 10^{10} \div 10^6$ megawatts
    $= 6 \cdot 5 \times 10^4$ megawatts

More help or practice

Millions ► Book R1 page 71

Positive powers of ten ► Book R1 pages 72 to 73

Standard index form ► Book R1 pages 73 to 75

Use of exponent key ► Book R1 pages 75 to 76

The rules of indices ► Book YR+ pages 29 to 30

Negative powers ► Book R1 pages 132 to 134

Mixed number (page 20)

1 (a) 100 g contains 22·1 g of fat.
        450 g contains $(22·1 \times 4·5)$g $= 99·45$ g
        $= 99·5$ g (to 1 d.p.)

   (b) 75% of 99·45 g $= 74·5875$ g
        $= 74·6$ g (to 1 d.p.)

2 (a) Advertising costs $= £2·50 - £1 - £0·25 - £0·75$
        $= £0·50$ or 50p

   (b) (i) $\dfrac{\text{Profit}}{\text{Total cost}} = \dfrac{\cancel{75}^{3}}{\cancel{250}_{10}} = \dfrac{3}{10}$

        (ii) $\frac{3}{10} = 0·3$

        (iii) $0·3 \times 100\% = 30\%$

3 (a) Total number $= (78 \times 2) + 42$
        $= 156 + 42$
        $= 198$

   (b) (i) $\dfrac{\text{Rooms occupied}}{\text{Rooms available}} = \dfrac{90}{120} = \dfrac{3}{4}$

        (ii) Total charge $= £(56 \times 83) + £(34 \times 54)$
              $= £6484$

        (iii) Number of people $= (56 \times 2) + 34 = 146$
              Percentage occupation $= \frac{146}{198} \times 100\%$
              $= 73·7\%$ (to 3 s.f.)

4 22 and 33

5 (a) $9·5 \times 10^{12}$ km

   (b) Distance in km $= 9·5 \times 10^{12} \times 4·3$
        $= 40·85 \times 10^{12}$
        $= 4·085 \times 10^{13}$

   (c) $(4·085 \times 10^{13}) \div (1·5 \times 10^{8}) = 2·72 \times 10^{5}$ (to 3 s.f.)

6 (a) 64
   (b) 0·015625
   (c) $n = 5$

7 (a) *Here are two methods of answering this question.*
        Decrease in candidates $= 151\,828 - 95\,000$
        $= 56\,828$
        Percentage decrease $= \frac{56\,828}{151\,828} \times 100\%$
        $= 37·4\%$ (to 3 s.f.)
        or
        Percentage decrease $= \left(100 - \frac{95\,000}{151\,828}\right)\%$
        $= (100 - 62·6)\%$
        $= 37·4\%$ (to 3 s.f.)

   (b) Number of examiners needed
        $\approx 150\,000 \times 2 \div 500$
        $= 300\,000 \div 500$
        $= 600$

        Any valid comments such as 'The exam board have got enough examiners' or 'There will be too many examiners'.

8 (a) *Work out the price per tumbler for each pack:*
        $£2·99 \div 3 \approx £1·00$ and $£6·99 \div 8 \approx £0·87$
        The 8-pack is the better value for money.

   (b) Any valid reason such as: a person living on their own wouldn't need eight glasses; or the purchaser couldn't afford to buy the larger pack.

ALGEBRA

Simplifying and substituting
(page 22)

More help or practice
Substituting values in expressions ► Book R1 pages 53 to 63, pages 89 to 92; Book R2 pages 20 to 21
Simplifying expressions ► Book R2 pages 104 to 108
Multiplying out brackets ► Book R2 pages 115 to 118
Substituting numbers into formulas
► Book R3 pages 119 to 120

1 (a) $5a$ (b) $3d + 2$

   (c) $n^2 + 2n$

     The expression cannot be simplified further.

   (d) $2ef + e + f$ *ef is the same as fe.*

   (e) $11c + 11d$ (f) $2a + 2b$ (g) $p + q + 3r$

   (h) $3m + mn + 2n$ (i) $-g - h$ or $^-g + {}^-h$

   Note that we usually put letters in alphabetical order.
   For example, we write $2ef + e + f$ and not $2fe + f + e$.
   It's not wrong if you don't do this, but it makes it easier
   to compare terms.

2 (a) $12a^2$ (b) a^2b (c) $10a^2b$ (d) $4x^2y^2$

   (e) a^2bc (f) $6a^3b$ (g) $4x^3y^2$ (h) $3a^2b^2c^2$

3 (a) x (b) $\frac{3xy}{5}$ or $\frac{3}{5}xy$ (c) $\frac{2x^2}{y^2}$ (d) $\frac{c^3}{ab^2}$

4 (a) $2x + 3y + 15$ (b) $7c - 3d$

   (c) $6a - b$ (d) $2y^2 - 10y$

   (e) $2x^2 - 7x$ (f) $^-6a^2 - 40a$

   (g) $6 - 3a + 2a^2$ (h) $5b^2 - 12b$

   (i) $x^2 + 3x + 3x - 12 = x^2 + 6x - 12$

5 (a) $3 + {}^-5 - 10 = {}^-12$

   (b) $(3)^2 + (^-5)^2 = 9 + 25 = 34$

   (c) $(3 \times 3) - 4(^-5) = 9 + 20 = 29$

   (d) $^-5(3 + 10) = {}^-65$

   (e) $3 + \left(\frac{10}{^-5}\right) = 3 + {}^-2 = 1$

   (f) $\frac{10 - {}^-5}{^-5} = \frac{15}{^-5} = 15 \div {}^-5 = {}^-3$

   (g) $3(3^2) = 3 \times 9 = 27$

   (h) $(3 \times 3)^2 = 9^2 = 81$

   (i) $\frac{1}{2}(3 + {}^-5) = \frac{1}{2} \times {}^-2 = {}^-1$

   (j) $^-2 \times 10^2 = {}^-200$

   (k) $(\frac{1}{2} \times 10) - {}^-5 = 5 - {}^-5 = 10$

   (l) $\frac{^-3}{4}(10 - 6) = \frac{^-3}{4} \times 4 = {}^-3$

Equations of straight line graphs
(page 24)

1   *Remember that the y-axis has equation x = 0 and*
   the x-axis has equation y = 0.

(a)

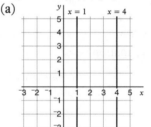

(b)

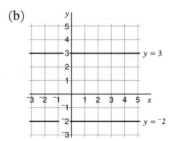

(c)

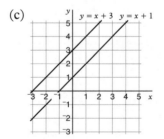

(d)

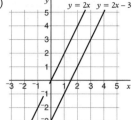

2 (a)

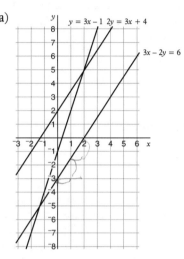

(b) (i) 3   (ii) $1\frac{1}{2}$ (iii) $1\frac{1}{2}$

3 $(6, 4)$, $(1, 0)$ and $(^-4, ^-4)$ lie on the line.

4 (a)

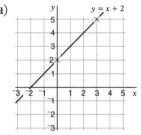

(b) The line cuts the y-axis at $(0, 2)$.

(c) $y = x + 2$

5 A: $y = x + 3$ B: $y = 3$

   C: $y = x$ D: $x = 2$

6 (a) The line has gradient $\frac{^-2}{3}$ and cuts
      the y-axis at $(0, 3)$.
      So its equation is $y = \frac{^-2}{3}x + 3$.

   (b) $y = \frac{^-2}{3}x + 6$

7 (a)

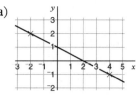

(b) The line has a gradient of $\frac{^-1}{2}$ or $^-0{\cdot}5$ and
   cuts the y-axis at $(0, 1)$.
   So its equation is $y = \frac{^-1}{2}x + 1$
   or $y = ^-0{\cdot}5x + 1$.

8 (a) $y = \frac{1}{2}x - 1$ or $2y = x - 2$

   (b) $y = \frac{^-4}{3}x + 4$ or $3y = ^-4x + 12$ or
      $4x + 3y = 12$

More help or practice

Drawing straight line graphs ► Book R+ pages 16 to 19

Gradients ► Book R2 pages 46 to 49, 74 to 76

Solving linear equations (page 26)

*After solving any equation it is important to check your
answer by substituting your solution back into the original
equation.*

1 (a) $x = 5$

   (b) $a = \frac{1}{2}$ or $0{\cdot}5$

   (c) $x = ^-3$
      *Start by writing the equation as $3x = ^-9$.
      It pays to be especially careful with negative signs.*

   (d) $x = 5$

   (e) $x = 12$

   (f) $x = 6$

   (g) $x = 8$ *Start by multiplying out the brackets.*

   (h) $x = ^-1$

2 (a) $1{\cdot}7x = 17{\cdot}7$, so $x = 10{\cdot}41$ (to 2 d.p.)

   (b) $29{\cdot}6 = 4a$, so $a = 7{\cdot}40$

   (c) $x = 4{\cdot}3 \times 7{\cdot}1 = 30{\cdot}53$

3 (a) $x = {}^-2\frac{1}{2}$

(b) $x = {}^-2\frac{1}{2}$ *Start by multiplying out the brackets.*

(c) $x = {}^-16$

(d) $x = {}^-4$ (e) $p = 3$ (f) $x = {}^-10\cdot5$

(g) $x = 3$ (h) $m = 28$ (i) $x = 8$

> **More help or practice**
>
> Solving linear equations with x on one side
> ► Book R2 pages 16 to 19
> Solving linear equations with x on both sides
> ► Book R2 page 22
> Solving equations with brackets ► Book R2 page 119

Brackets and factors (page 27)

1 (a) $2x + 8 = 2(x + 4)$

(b) $3a - 12b = 3(a - 4b)$

(c) $4x + xy = x(4 + y)$

(d) $4x + 20y = 4(x + 5y)$

(e) $x^2 + 4x = x(x + 4)$

(f) $8ab - 12b = 4b(2a - 3)$

(g) $^-x^2 - 3x = {}^-x(x + 3)$

(h) $^-5n^2 - 30n = {}^-5n(n + 6)$

(i) $^-2x^2 + 4x = {}^-2x(x - 2)$

2 (a) $5(a + 4b)$ (b) $a(4 + b)$ (c) $n(n + 3)$

(d) $2x(1 + 3x)$ (e) $4y(2x + 3)$ (f) $4x(x - 3)$

(g) $4n(m - 2n)$ (h) $^-x(x - 2)$ or $x(^-x + 2)$

3 (a) $4a^2 \times 4a^2 = 16a^4$

(b) $2a^3 \times 2a^3 = 4a^6$

(c) $2x^3 + 3x^2 = x^2(2x + 3)$

(d) $2x^{2+1} = 2x^3$ *Note that $x = x^1$.*

(e) $5c^{4-1} = 5c^3$

(f) $3c^{5-3} = 3c^2$

(g) $6x^{2+3} = 6x^5$

(h) $3 \times 2x^2 \times 2x^2 \times 2x^2 = 24x^6$

4 *There are many different answers. Here are some.*

(a) $ab + 23ab$, $3a \times 8b$, $8a \times 3b$, $24 \times ab$, $12a \times 2b$, and so on

(b) $24 \times ab \times a$, $12ab \times 2a$, $3a^2 \times 8b$, $2a \times 12ab$, ...

(c) $25 \times x^3$, $5x^2 \times 5x$, $25x^2 \times x$, $24x^3 + x^3$, ...

> **More help or practice**
>
> Multiplying out brackets ► Book R2 pages 115 to 118, 121
> Factorising simple expressions ► Book R2 pages 122 to 123
> The rules of indices ► Book YR+ pages 29 to 30

Time graphs (page 28)

1 (a) (i) 25   (ii) 100   (iii) 0

(b) 200 metres

(c) The girl walks towards the bus-stop for 4 minutes, sees the bus coming, and runs for 1 minute but misses the bus. She waits for 3 minutes before another bus arrives. She gets on and the bus drives off at 400 m per minute.

2 (a) The cold water tap was turned on.

(b) Both taps were turned off.

(c) The plug was pulled out.

3 (a) The car is travelling at a constant speed.

(b) The car is slowing down and finally stops.

(c) The car speeds up (accelerates) fast at first and then more gently, before travelling at a constant speed.

4

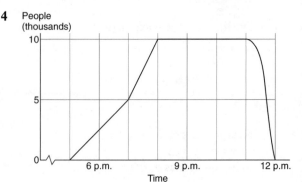

5 (a)

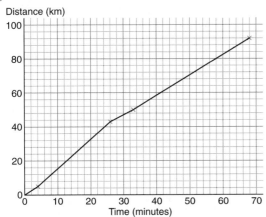

Distance (km) / Time (minutes)

(b) The fastest part of the journey is between Finsbury Park and Stevenage.

(c) The average speed for this part of the journey is given by
$(38 \div 22)$ km/min $= 1.7$ km/min (to 2 s.f.).

More help or practice

Reading and drawing graphs ► Book B2 pages 45 to 52

Constant rates ► Book R2 pages 90 to 92

Changes in rates ► Book R2 pages 94 to 97

Drawing and using non-linear graphs
(page 30)

1 (a)

x	$^-2$	$^-1$	0	1	2	3	4	5
$x^2 - 3x$	10	4	0	$^-2$	$^-2$	0	4	10
$^-x^2 + 3x$	$^-10$	$^-4$	0	2	2	0	$^-4$	$^-10$

(b)

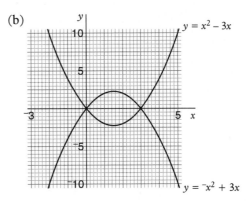

$y = x^2 - 3x$

$y = ^-x^2 + 3x$

Each graph is a reflection of the other in the x-axis.

If your graphs are different from these you have probably made a slip in your table of values. Negative numbers need special care.

2 (a)

x	$^-4$	$^-3$	$^-2$	$^-1$	0	1	2	3	4
y	65	40	21	8	1	0	5	16	33

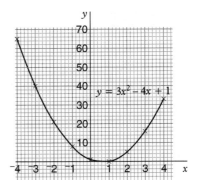

$y = 3x^2 - 4x + 1$

(b)

x	$^-3$	$^-2$	$^-1$	0	1	2	3
y	$^-27$	$^-8$	$^-1$	0	1	8	27

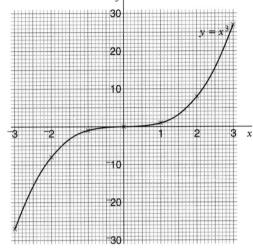

(c)

x	$^-6$	$^-4$	$^-3$	$^-2$	$^-1$	1	2	3	4	6
y	$^-2$	$^-3$	$^-4$	$^-6$	$^-12$	12	6	4	3	2

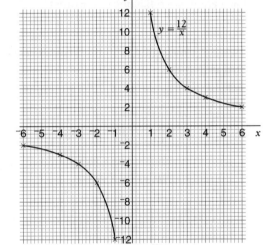

3 (a) and (b)

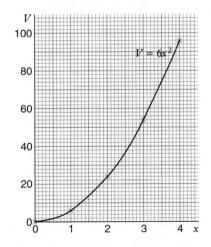

(b) (i) The accurate answer is $37 \cdot 5 \, \text{m}^3$, but you would gain full marks for an answer between $36 \, \text{m}^3$ and $39 \, \text{m}^3$.

(ii) Any value between $1 \cdot 8 \, \text{m}$ and $1 \cdot 9 \, \text{m}$.

4 (a) The missing values of V are 10 and $2 \cdot 5$.

(b)

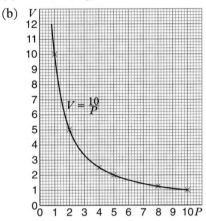

(c) $V \approx 3 \cdot 3 \, \text{cm}^3$

(d) As P gets larger and larger, V becomes smaller and smaller. V gets closer and closer to zero but never quite reaches it.

5 (a) When $t = 3$ seconds, $h = 45$ metres.

(b)

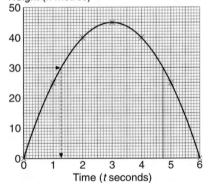

(c) When $h = 30 \, \text{m}$, $t = 1 \cdot 3 \, \text{s}$ (or $4 \cdot 7 \, \text{s}$).

6 (a) The missing values of l are 32 and 50.

(b) Length (l metres)

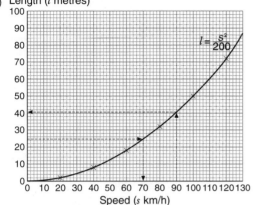

(c) The skid is between 40 m and 41 m long.

(d) The speed is between 69 km/h and 70 km/h.

More help or practice

Substituting numbers into formulas
► Book R3 pages 119 to 120

Drawing graphs from formulas ► Book R3 pages 120 to 123

Drawing the graphs of $y = ax^2$, $y = ax^3$ and $y = \frac{a}{x}$
► Book Y5 pages 73 to 74

Graphical solution of equations ► Book R3 page 123

Changing the subject of a formula (page 33)

1 (a) $w = e - 5$ (b) $a = b + 3$

(c) $d = \dfrac{C}{\pi}$ (d) $2e = l - 5$, so $e = \dfrac{l-5}{2}$

(e) $mx = y - c$, so $x = \dfrac{y-c}{m}$

(f) $h(a + b) = 2A$, so $h = \dfrac{2A}{a+b}$

(g) $RI = V$, so $I = \dfrac{V}{R}$

(h) $2s = t(u + v)$, so $2s = tu + tv$

$$tv = 2s - tu$$

and $v = \dfrac{2s - tu}{t}$ or $\dfrac{2s}{t} - u$

2 *Here are two ways of making the rearrangement.*

$L = 4(2a + b)$ or $L = 4(2a + b)$

$\dfrac{L}{4} = 2a + b$ $L = 8a + 4b$

$b = \dfrac{L}{4} - 2a$ $L - 8a = 4b$

$\dfrac{L - 8a}{4} = b$

Both answers would be given full marks.

3 $V = \dfrac{W}{A}$, so $AV = W$ and $A = \dfrac{W}{V}$

4 $C = 120 + 40n$, so $40n = C - 120$

and $n = \dfrac{C - 120}{40}$ or $\dfrac{C}{40} - 3$

5 (a) $h = \dfrac{2V}{bl}$ (b) $h = \dfrac{2 \times 24}{2 \cdot 5 \times 8} = \dfrac{48}{20} = 2 \cdot 4$

More help or practice

Changing the subject of a formula
► Book R2 pages 42 to 45, pages 57 to 58

Inequalities and regions (page 34)

1 (a) $x > 3$ (b) $x \geq 7$

(c) $a > {}^{-}2$

Note the change in the 'direction' of the inequality sign.

(d) $b < 15$ (e) $a \leq 3$ (f) $c > {}^{-}5$

(g) $x \leq 6$ *Multiply both sides by 2.*

(h) $5x + 5 > 2x + 14$, so $3x > 9$ and $x > 3$

2 (a) ${}^{-}2$, ${}^{-}1$, 0, 1 and 2

(b) ${}^{-}2$, ${}^{-}1$, 0, 1, 2 and 3

3 6, 8, 10, 12 and 14

4 The two inequalities are
$3x - 2 > 47$ and $3x - 2 < 62$.
Solving these gives $x > 16\frac{1}{3}$ and $x < 21\frac{1}{3}$.
So Ajaz could have thought of 17, 18, 19, 20 or 21.

5 (a) $n + n + 1 + n + 2 < 48$
$3n < 45$
$n < 15$

(b) The three largest possible numbers are 14, 15 and 16.

6 The three inequalities and their solutions are:

(i) $2x < (x+1) + (2-x)$
$2x < 3$
$x < \frac{3}{2}$

(ii) $(2-x) < (x+1) + 2x$
$2-x < 3x+1$
$1 < 4x$ or $4x > 1$
so $x > \frac{1}{4}$

(iii) $(x+1) < 2x + (2-x)$
$x+1 < 2x + 2 - x$
$1 < 2$

7 *First write the inequality as two separate inequalities.*
$1 \le 2-x$ which gives $x \le 1$
and $2-x < 4$ which gives $x > {}^-2$.
Values of x which fit both these are ${}^-1, 0$ and 1.

8 (a) $y > x$ (b) $y > 2$ (c) $y + x < 2$

9 (a)

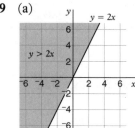

(b)

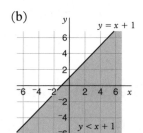

(c)

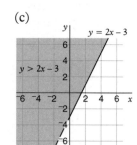

(d)

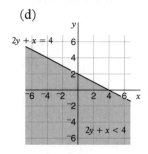

More help or practice

Inequalities ► Book R+ pages 10 to 12

Solving inequalities ► Book R+ pages 13 to 15

Representing inequalities as a region on a graph
► Book Y2 pages 123 to 125, Book Y5 pages 121 to 126

Simultaneous equations (page 36)

1 (a)

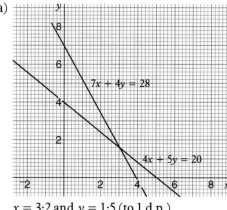

(b) The coordinates of the point where the two lines cross give the solution to the equations: $x \approx 0.6$ and $y \approx 2.1$.
(The exact solutions are $x = 0.57$ and $y = 2.14$.)

2 (a)

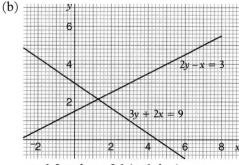

$x = 3.2$ and $y = 1.5$ (to 1 d.p.)

(b)

$x = 1.3$ and $y = 2.1$ (to 1 d.p.)

Did you draw these lines by finding where they cut the x- and y-axes?

3 $4y + 5x = 20$ $2x - y = 0$

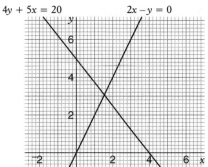

$x = 1.5$ and $y = 3.1$ (to 1 d.p.)

4   *For this question you could plot a against b or b against a.*
Providing you are consistent it does not matter.

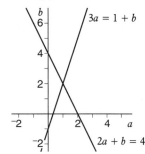

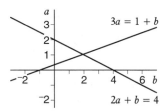

$a = 1$ and $b = 2$

5 $x = 2, y = 3$
Remember to check that these values satisfy the original
equations.

6   (a) $x = 1$ and $y = 3$ (b) $x = 2$ and $y = 3$
    (c) $x = 1$ and $y = ^-2$ (d) $x = ^-2$ and $y = 6$
    (e) $x = 3$ and $y = ^-0.5$ (f) $x = 3$ and $y = ^-2$
    (g) $x = ^-2$ and $y = 1.5$ (h) $a = 2$ and $b = 1$

7   The lines meet at the point $(2, 3)$.

More help or practice

Graphical solution ► Book R+ pages 20 to 23
Algebraic solution ► Book YR+ pages 6 to 11

Recognising graphs (page 38)

1   (a) y is proportional to x in (ii).
    There are two ways of answering this question:
    Plot the values and find which one(s) lie on a
    straight line passing through the origin.
    or
    Look carefully at the numbers, checking that if
    one number is zero, the other is zero as well, and
    that the ratio of x to y remains the same.
    (b) $y = 1.2x$ or $y = \frac{6}{5}x$

2   (a) The bath is filling at 20 litres/minute.
       Notice that this is the gradient of the graph.
    (b) $V = 20t$.
       Always check that your equation is true for two
       points on the line.

3   (a) The missing values are $m = 1.8$ and $F = 1.5$.
    (b) (i) The gradient is 3.
        (ii) $F = 3m$

4   (a) and (b)

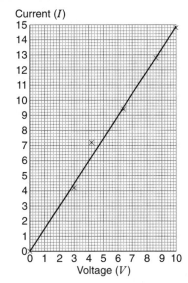

Your line should start exactly at (0, 0).

    (c) The gradient of the graph is 1.5 (or between
       1.4 and 1.6).
    (d) $I = 1.5V$

5

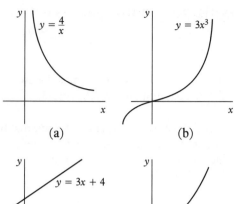

(a)   (b)

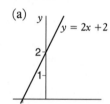
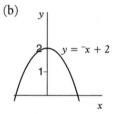

(c)   (d)

6 With questions like these it is usually a good idea to check your answers by substituting known values back into the equation.

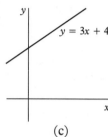
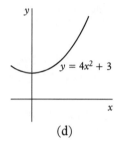

(a)   (b)

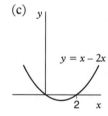
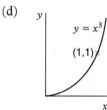

(c)   (d)

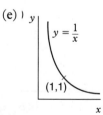

(e)

More help or practice
Proportionality ► Book R2 pages 69 to 74
Approximate proportionality ► Book R2 pages 77 to 78
Recognising graphs ► Book Y5 pages 74 to 75

Trial and improvement; graphical solution (page 40)

1 *Always show all your trials. You may get some marks for this even if your final answer is wrong.*
Here are some trials. You may have needed a few more.

Trial value of x	Value of $x^3 - 2x^2$
2	0
3	9
2·5	3·125
2·3	1·587
2·4	2·304
2·35	1·932 875

The solution must lie between 2·4 and 2·35, which is 2·4 (to 2 s.f.).

2 (a) $x^3 + 5x = 69·153$

  (b) *Here are some trials. You may have needed more.*

Trial value of x	Value of $x^3 + 5x$
3·6	64·656
3·5	60·375
3·4	56·304
3·48	59·544 192
3·49	59·958 549

3·49 was only a check, as 3·48 was enough.

The solution is between 3·50 and 3·49.
So $x = 3·5$ (to 1 d.p.)

3 $x = 3·42$ correct to 2 decimal places.
Remember to show all your trials. The key trials are 3·42 and 3·415.

4 (a)

x	⁻3	⁻2	⁻1	0	1	2	3
y	9	4	1	0	1	4	9

(b) and (c)

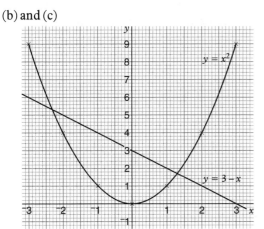

(d) $x = {}^{-}2 \cdot 3$ or $1 \cdot 3$

5 (a) The missing values are ⁻1, 8, 4, 2, 1·6, 1·3, 1·1, 1.

Notice the pattern in the table of values, which is a useful check.

(b) and (c) (i)

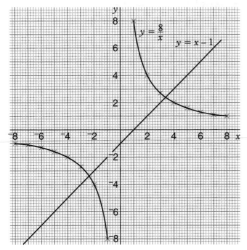

(c) (ii) $x = {}^{-}2 \cdot 4$ or $x = 3 \cdot 4$ (to 1 d.p.)

6 (a) The missing values are 3, 1·25 and 3.

Notice the symmetry in the table as a check on your graph.

(b)

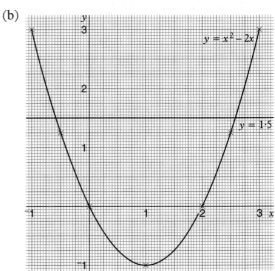

(c) $x = 2 \cdot 6$ and $x = {}^{-}0 \cdot 6$

These are the x-coordinates of the points where the curve cuts the line $y = 1 \cdot 5$.

> **More help or practice**
> Trial and improvement ► Book R+ pages 28 to 32
> Using graphs to solve equations ► Book R3 page 123

Setting up expressions and equations (page 42)

With questions like these remember that your unknown represents a number only, not a number and a unit. Always check your answer by substitution in the **original** *question, not your equation, in case you got it wrong.*

1 (a) The number $+ x = 7$, so the number $= 7 - x$.

(b) The sum of the bottom numbers is $14 - y$.

2 $3(a - 2)$ or $3 \times (a - 2)$ or $(a - 2) \times 3$ or $3a - 6$

3 Let x represent Scott's number.
$$4x - 7 = 3x + 8$$
$$x = 15$$

4 (a) The three consecutive numbers are $(n-1), n$ and $(n+1)$.
Examples of three consecutive numbers are: 2, 3, 4 and 76, 77, 78.

(b) The sum of $(n-1), n$ and $(n+1)$ is $n-1+n+n+1 = 3n$
This will always be divisible by three.

5 Let $x°$ be the third angle.
Then $a+b+x = 180$, so $x = 180-a-b$.

6 (a) Let x be the original number.
Carrying out the instructions gives
$7x + 13 = 69$.

(b) The solution to $7x + 13 = 69$ is $x = 8$.

7 Let x be the number of sheep in one flock.
The other flock will have $2x - 20$ sheep.
The total number of sheep is $x + (2x - 20)$.
You need to solve the equation $3x - 20 = 244$
$$3x = 264$$
$$x = 88$$
So the numbers of sheep in the flocks are 88 and 156.

8 (a) $(420 - x)$ tickets were not booked in advance.

(b) Money in £ from advance bookings $= x \times 5$
Money in £ taken at the door $= (420 - x) \times 8$
But £2460 was taken in total.
So $5x + 8(420 - x) = 2460$
$^-3x + 3360 = 2460$ which simplifies to
$$3x = 900.$$
Any form of the equation would gain full marks.

(c) Solving $3x = 900$ gives $x = 300$, the number of advance bookings.

9 The perimeter in units is $2(x+x+3) = 24$
$$4x + 6 = 24$$
$$4x = 18$$
$$x = 4\tfrac{1}{2} \text{ or } 4\cdot5$$

10 (a) (i) $(36 \times x) + (12 \times y)$ or $36x + 12y$
(ii) $(100 \times x) + (80 \times y)$ or $100x + 80y$

(b) $36x + 12y \geq 240$ and $100x + 80y \leq 1000$
These simplify to $3x + y \geq 20$ and $5x + 4y \leq 50$, but you would get full marks for the inequalities above.

11 (a) $5x > 90$

(b) $a + b + 6 \geq 60$, so $a + b \geq 54$ (or $54 \leq a + b$)
'At least' means 'greater than or equal to'.

(c) $10x \leq 100$, so $x \leq 10$ (or $10 \geq x$)
'Cannot be more than' means must be 'less than or equal to'.

12 (a) The height (in cm) of 6 chairs
$= 68 + (5 \times 9) = 113$

(b) $h = 68 + 9 \times (c - 1) = 9c + 59$

(c) Solving $9c + 59 = 196$ gives $c = 15\cdot222\ldots$
So the greatest number chairs which will fit through a 196 cm high doorway is 15.

More help or practice
Problems leading to formulas and equations
► Book R2 page 120, Book R3 pages 59 to 61

Quadratics (page 44)

1 (a) $x^2 + 3x + 2$ (b) $x^2 - x - 20$
(c) $x^2 - 9x + 20$ (d) $a^2 - 4$
(e) $2x^2 + 9x + 4$ (f) $6x^2 - 5x - 6$
(g) $12x^2 - 29x + 15$ (h) $30a^2 + 34a - 8$

2 (a) $x^2 + 4x + 4$ (b) $x^2 - 4x + 4$
(c) $4x^2 + 4x + 1$ (d) $a^2 + 2ab + b^2$

3 (a) $(x + 3)(x + 4)$ (b) $(x + 3)(x + 7)$
(c) $(x - 3)(x + 5)$ (d) $(x + 4)(x + 5)$
(e) $(x - 2)(x - 4)$ (f) $(x - 1)(x + 7)$

4 (a) If $x(x - 3) = 0$, then $x = 0$ or $x = 3$.

(b) If $(x - 2)(x + 7) = 0$, then $x = 2$ or $x = {^-}7$.

(c) If $(x + 2)(x - 9) = 0$, then $x = {^-}2$ or $x = 9$.

5 (a) $x(x + 2) = 0$,   so $x = 0$ or $^-2$
(b) $x(2x + 1) = 0$,   so $x = 0$ or $\frac{-1}{2}$
(c) $(x - 5)(x + 4) = 0$,   so $x = 5$ or $^-4$
(d) $(x - 4)(x - 2) = 0$,   so $x = 4$ or 2
(e) $(x + 5)(x - 2) = 0$,   so $x = {^-}5$ or 2

(f) $(x + 6)(x + 4) = 0$, so $x = {}^-6$ or ${}^-4$

(g) $(x + 5)(x - 1) = 0$, so $x = {}^-5$ or 1

(h) $(x + 5)(x - 4) = 0$, so $x = {}^-5$ or 4

(i) $(x - 7)(x - 3) = 0$, so $x = 7$ or 3

In (j), (k) and (l) start by writing the equations in the usual form.

(j) $x^2 + 7x + 10 = 0$
$(x + 5)(x + 2) = 0$, so $x = {}^-5$ or ${}^-2$

(k) $x^2 - x - 12 = 0$
$(x - 4)(x + 3) = 0$, so $x = 4$ or ${}^-3$

(l) $x^2 - 12x - 13 = 0$
$(x - 13)(x + 1) = 0$, so $x = 13$ or ${}^-1$

6 (a) There are two ways of dividing the plan, but both give the same expression for the area:

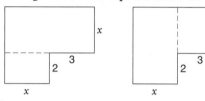

$x(3 + x) + 2x$ 　　　 $x(2 + x) + 3x$
$= x^2 + 5x$ 　　　　　 $= x^2 + 5x$

(b) You need to solve the equation
$x^2 + 5x = 24$.

$x^2 + 5x - 24 = 0$
$(x + 8)(x - 3) = 0$
$x = {}^-8$ or 3

The only value which has a meaning is $x = 3$.

7 (a) Area (in m^2) is $(x + 4)(x - 2)$.

(b) *To find the value of x you need to solve the equation $(x + 4)(x - 2) = 40$. Start by removing the brackets and re-writing the equation in a form to factorise it.*
$x^2 + 2x - 8 = 40$
$x^2 + 2x - 48 = 0$
$(x + 8)(x - 6) = 0$
$x = {}^-8$ or 6

The only value which 'makes sense' is $x = 6$.

More help or practice

Multiplying out double brackets ► Book Y2 page 48

Factorising a quadratic equation ► Book Y4 pages 147 to 148

Sequences and terms (page 46)

1 $5, 8, 11, 14, 17$ and 20

2 (a) 12 and $2n$

(b) 9 and $3 + n$

(c) 18 and $2(3 + n)$ or $6 + 2n$
Compare this with the sequence in (b).

(d) 11 and $2n - 1$ 　 *Look at sequence (a).*

(e) 36 and n^2 　 *It pays to recognise square numbers!*

(f) 37 and $n^2 + 1$ 　 *See the previous sequence.*

3 (a)

(b)

Pattern	...	4	5	6
Unshaded	...	16	20	24
Shaded	...	17	21	25

(c) $5 + (n - 1) \times 4$ or $4n + 1$

4 (a) $50, 72$ and 98 　 2×5^2, 2×6^2, 2×7^2

(b) $2n^2$ *(not $(2n)^2$)*

Sequences in which the difference between terms does not remain the same usually suggest that a square number is involved.

5 $b = 2g + 2$

If you had difficulties, look at the way the pattern is built up.

More help or practice

Patterns and sequences ► Book RB+ pages 12 to 16

Sequences and formulas ► Book RB+ pages 17 to 19, Book YR+ pages 38 to 41

Finding and stating rules ► Book R3 pages 57 to 59

Mixed algebra (page 47)

1 (a) $4n + 20 \leq 50$

(b) Solving this inequality gives $n \leq 7\frac{1}{2}$.
The largest number of packs is 7.

2 (a) $P = 4H - 5$

(b) (i) $3x - 5 = 7 - x$
$$3x = 12 - x$$
$$4x = 12$$
$$x = 3$$

(ii) $\frac{1}{2}x + 2 = 1$
$$x + 4 = 2$$
$$x = {}^{-}2$$

3

Trial value	Value of x^3
$x = 2\cdot2$	$10\cdot648$
$x = 2\cdot4$	$13\cdot824$
$x = 2\cdot5$	$15\cdot625$
$x = 2\cdot45$	$14\cdot706\,125$
$x = 2\cdot46$	$14\cdot886\,936$
$x = 2\cdot47$	$15\cdot069\,223$
$x = 2\cdot465$	$14\cdot977\,895$

So x must lie between $2\cdot465$ and $2\cdot47$, which means
that $x = 2\cdot47$ (to 2 d.p.).

Remember to check your answer.

4 (a) The missing values are 3, 7, 19, 28 and 39.

(b)

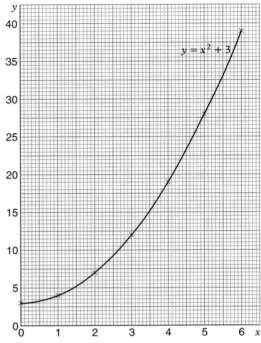

(c) When $y = 30$, $x = 5\cdot2$

5 (a) The next two terms are 41 and 122.

(b) (i) The next two terms are 16 and 22.
(ii) Add 11 to the 11th term.

6 (a) The missing numbers are 34 and 43.

(b) $y = 9x - 2$

(c) If $y = 9x - 2$ then $y + 2 = 9x$, so $x = \dfrac{y + 2}{9}$.

SHAPE, SPACE AND MEASURES

Understanding shape (page 48)

1 (a) (i) 1   (ii) 2

    (b) (i) 2   (ii) 4

2 (a) Your own full-size drawing

It is probably easiest to draw triangle EFD first, then the other three triangles. Notice that the centre of the circle is where CF and BE meet.

    (b) Radius = 7·0 or 7·1 cm

3 (a) Your own drawing   (b) Angle C = 90°

4 Your own drawing

5 (a) Your own drawing   (b) 6·6 cm

6 (a) (i) 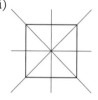 (ii)

    (b) (i) 4   (ii) 3

7 (a) H, I, J, K

    (b) A, B and H, I, J, K

      Equilateral triangles are also isosceles.

    (c) D, F, G

    (d) D   *Rhombus D is also a parallelogram.*

    (e) H, I, K

    (f) E   *Reflected shapes are still congruent.*

8 (a) There 4 possible answers.

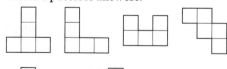

    (b)   (c)

9

Rectangle	No	2	2
Rhombus	**Yes**	**2**	**2**
Parallelogram	**No**	**0**	**2**
Kite	**Yes**	**1**	**1**
Square	**Yes**	**4**	**4**

10 (a)

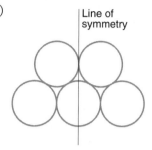

Line of symmetry

    (b) (i), (ii)

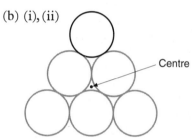

Centre

       (iii) 120°

    (c) (i)

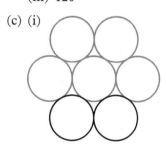

       (ii) 60°

    (d)

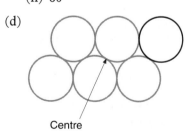

Centre

The circle could go at the other end.

11 (a)

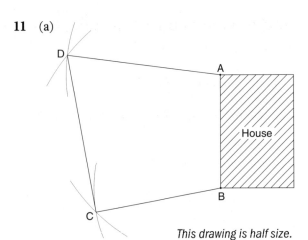

This drawing is half size.

(b) Between 47 and 49 metres

More help or practice

Reflection symmetry in two dimensions
► Book B1 pages 8 to 9, 74 to 77; Book B+ page 24

Rotation symmetry in two dimensions
► Book B1 pages 10 to 14, 78 to 82; Book B+ page 25

Construction of a triangle given the sides ► Book R2 pages 64 to 65

Reflection and rotation symmetry in three dimensions
► Book B+ pages 49 to 55

Congruency ► Book YR+ pages 14 to 18

Angles (page 51)

1 (a) $a = 30°$ (angles on a straight line)

(b) $b = 72°$ (angle sum of a triangle)

2 (a) (i) $x = 180° - (360° \div 5) = 108°$
(ii) $y = 36°$ *Triangle ABE is isosceles.*
(iii) $z = 108° - y = 72°$

(b) *You could give two different reasons here.*
BE is parallel to CD because the pentagon is symmetrical about the line through A perpendicular to CD.
or
Angle BED $= 72°$, and angle EDC $= 108°$, so the lines are parallel, as the interior angles add up to $180°$.

3 (a) $2p + 125° + 95° = 360°$ (angle sum of a quadrilateral)
$2p = 360° - 125° - 95° = 140°$
$p = 70°$

(b) $q = 360° - 95° = 265°$ (angles at a point)

4 *Notice that the two marks on the sides of the right-hand triangle mean that those sides are equal.*
Also, you are not required to find angle w, even though it is marked on the diagram (to show you which angle to find first).

(a) $w = 180° - 80°$
$x = 180° - w - 45°$
$= 35°$

(b) $y = 180° - 80° - x = 180° - 115° = 65°$

(c) $2z + (180° - 2x) = 180°$ *Isosceles triangle*
$2z - 70 = 0$
$z = 35°$

5 $a = 180° - 122° = 58°$
$b = 85°$ $b + 37° = 122°$
$c = 37°$ *Alternate (Z) angles*
$d = 180° - c = 143°$

6 (a) $x = 90° \div 2 = 45°$
Triangle is isosceles and right-angled – angle in a semicircle

(b) $y = 50°$ *Isosceles triangle*
$z = 40°$ *Large triangle is right-angled*

7 (a) Angle AFE $= 180° - (360° \div 6) = 120°$

(b) Angle GFE $= 180° - (360° \div 8) = 135°$

(c) *Notice in this part of the question that 'produced' means 'extended'.*
XFY $=$ AFG
$= 360° -$ AFE $-$ GFE
$= 105°$

8 (a) Triangle ABE is isosceles, so angle BEA $= x$.
So $2x + 42° = 180°$.
and $x = 69°$

(b) $y + 74° = 180°$ *BE is parallel to CD.*
$y = 106°$

9 (a) Angle CDF $= 25°$

*AB is parallel to DC (opposite sides of a rectangle),
so BAC = ACD (alternate (Z) angles).
AC is parallel to DF, so ACD = CDF
(alternate (Z) angles).*

(b) DEF $= 130°$

*EFD = CDF (alternate (Z) angles, since DC is
parallel to EF – opposite sides of a rhombus).
FDE = EFD (triangle EFD is isosceles – DE = EF
as they are sides of a rhombus).
DEF = 180° – EFD – FDE (angle sum of a triangle).*

10 (a) Angle CDB $= 60°$ (angles on a straight line)
Angle ABD $= 90°$ (tangent)
Angle BAD $= 30°$ (angle sum of a triangle)

(b) Angle ACB $= 90°$ (angle in a semi-circle)
Angle BCD $= 90°$ (angles on a straight line)
Angle CBD $= 30°$ (angle sum of a triangle)

More help or practice

Basic angle properties ► Book B2 pages 60 to 65,
Book R2 pages 23 to 25

Corresponding angles (F-angles) ► Book R2 pages 26 to 27,
Book RB+ pages 27 to 28

Alternate angles (Z-angles) ► Book R2 pages 28 to 30

Angles of a quadrilateral ► Book R2 page 31

Angle in a semicircle ► Book Y4 page 28

Names and properties of polygons
► Book B+ pages 15 to 17, 20 to 23, 62 to 65

Calculating angles of regular polygons
► Book B2 pages 66 to 68, Book B+ pages 18 to 19

Length, area and volume 1 (page 54)

1 (a) $\frac{1}{2} \times 2 \cdot 5 \times (4 + 2)\,\text{cm}^2 = 7 \cdot 5\,\text{cm}^2$

Make sure you include the units.

(b) $10 \cdot 5\,\text{cm}^2$ or $10 \cdot 4\,\text{cm}^2$

*Notice that you could work this out in two ways –
either $4 \times 2 \cdot 6 = 10 \cdot 4$ or $3 \times 3 \cdot 5 = 10 \cdot 5$.
The two answers are slightly different, but both
would gain full marks.*

2 Total volume in $\text{cm}^3 = (10 \times 10 \times 3) + (10 \times 5 \times 3)$
$$= 450$$

3 $120\,\text{m}$ *One side is $\sqrt{900\,m} = 30\,m$.*

4 Total length $= (\frac{1}{2}\pi \times 78 + 132 \cdot 5)\,\text{cm}$
$$= 255\,\text{cm}$$

5 $73\,\text{m}$ (to 2 s.f.)

*AB is the diameter of a circle with circumference $400\,m$.
So $\pi \times AB = 400$ and $AB = 127 \cdot 32\,m$.*

6 (a) $0 \cdot 576\,\text{g}$ $(56 - 18) \div 66$

Notice that the width of the tape does not matter.

(b) Circumference of Earth $= (2\pi \times 6400)\,\text{km}$
$$= 40\,212\,\text{km}$$
1 m of tape weighs $0 \cdot 575\,75$ g, so
1 km weighs $(0 \cdot 575\,75 \times 1000)\text{g} = 575 \cdot 75\,\text{g}$
$$= 0 \cdot 575\,75\,\text{kg}.$$
So total weight is $40\,212 \times 0 \cdot 575\,75\,\text{kg}$
$= 23\,152 \cdot 059\,\text{kg}$
$= 23\,000\,\text{kg}$ (to 2 s.f.)

More help or practice

Volume of a cuboid ► Book R1 page 3

Circumference of a circle ► Book B2 pages 102 to 108,
Book R2 pages 132 to 133

Area of a parallelogram and triangle ► Book R2 pages 60 to 63

Area of a trapezium ► Book R2 pages 65 to 68

Surface area of a cuboid ► Book R+ page 3

Representing three dimensions
(page 56)

All these answers are drawn half size.

1 (a)

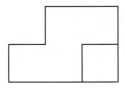

  (b)

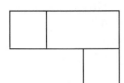

  (c)

2 (a)

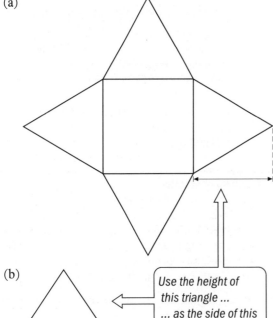

  (b)

Use the height of
this triangle ...
... as the side of this
triangle.

5 cm

  (c) 3·5 cm
    The height of the pyramid is the height of the
    triangle in part (b).

3 (a) 1·5 cm by 4 cm by 1·5 cm   *(any order)*

  (b)

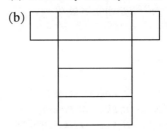

  *Many other nets are possible, but you should have
  4 rectangles, each 4 cm by 1·5 cm, and two
  1·5 cm squares; they must join together sensibly.*

4 *Notice that the
  diagram in the
  question is rather
  misleading – the
  1·25 m side looks
  shorter than the
  1·00 m side.*

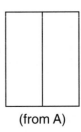

(from A)

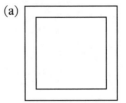

(from B)   (from C)

*The height of
the roof in C
is found from
your drawing
of B – shown
by the dotted
lines.*

5 (a)

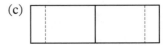

  (b) 7·1 cm

  (c)

Take the measurements from your plan in (a).

6 (a)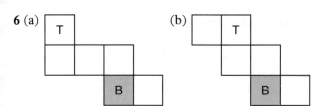

(b)

7

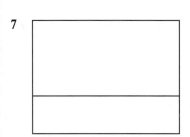

8 (a) *Half-size*

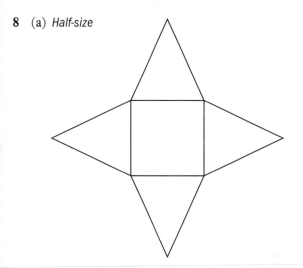

(b) 4·7 cm

More help or practice

Nets of a cube and cuboid ► Book R1 pages 1 and 2

Plans and elevations ► Book R2 pages 80 to 89

Units, measuring and compound measures (page 58)

1 (a) 170 cm

(b) 60 kg

(c) 450 cm²

(d) 200 ml

'Capacity' is another word for volume. It is usually used for containers that hold liquids.

2 3 litres = 3×100 cl = 300 cl
You can fill 300 cl ÷ 20 cl = 15 glasses.

3 (a) 18 in ≈ $18 \times 2\cdot5$ cm = 45 cm or 450 mm

(b) 4 gallons ≈ $4 \times 4\cdot5$ litres = 18 litres

(c) 5 feet 6 in = $(5 \times 12 + 6)$ in = 66 in
66 in ≈ $66 \times 2\cdot5$ cm = 165 cm
(or 5 feet 6 in = $5\frac{1}{2}$ feet ≈ $5\frac{1}{2} \times 30$ cm = 165 cm)

4 8·90 m = 890 cm = $(890 \div 2\cdot54)$ in
= 350·3937 in = 350·5 in (to nearest $\frac{1}{2}$ in)
350 ÷ 12 = 29·16666 feet
29 feet = 29×12 inches = 348 inches
leaving 2·5 inches over from the 350·5 inches.
So his record is 29 feet $2\frac{1}{2}$ inches.

Notice that 'answer in feet and inches' means that you work out how many feet the length is, and how many inches are left over.

5 To measure a 10 cm line in metres seems unnecessary. Centimetres are the better unit. Sasha's answer is 10·3 cm, which appears to be measured to the nearest mm, which is reasonable.
Andy seems to be measuring to $\frac{1}{100}$ th cm or $\frac{1}{10}$ th mm. This is too accurate for their purposes, and impossible to do with ordinary instruments.

6 Time is between $12\cdot8 - \frac{1}{2} \times 0\cdot1 = 12\cdot75$ seconds
and $12\cdot8 + \frac{1}{2} \times 0\cdot1 = 12\cdot85$ seconds.

7 Average speed = 247 miles ÷ 4 hours
  = 61·75 m.p.h. = 62 m.p.h. (to the nearest whole number)

8 (a) Time taken = 264 ÷ 72 hours
    = 3·666 666 hours
    = 3·666 666 × 60 minutes
    = 219·999 99 minutes
    = 220 minutes

 (b) The faster train takes (220 − 22) minutes
    = 198 minutes = 3·3 hours
    So speed = 264 ÷ 3·3 km/h = 80 km/h

9 1 litre = 1000 ml = $1\frac{3}{4}$ pints

 So 1 pt = $1000 \div 1\frac{3}{4}$ ml = 571·428 57 ml

 1 pt = 20 fl oz, so 1 fl oz = 571·428 57 ÷ 20 ml
 = 28·571 428 ml
 So it needs 8 × 28·571 428 ml
 = 228·571 428 ml = 230 ml (to nearest 10 ml)

10 1·5 litres = 1500 ml
 1 ml of gold weighs 18·7 g, so 1500 ml
 will weigh (1500 × 18·7) g = 28 050 g
 = (28 050 ÷ 1000) kg = 28·05 kg
 = 28 kg (to 2 s.f.)
 An answer of 28·05 kg is a bit too accurate, since the crucible is unlikely to have a volume of exactly 1·5 litres.

More help or practice

Litres and millilitres ► Book R1 pages 4 and 5

Constant rates ► Book R2 pages 90 to 92

Average rates (including speed) ► Book R2 pages 93 to 98

Conversion between metric and Imperial units
► Book RB+ pages 20 to 24

Measurement and accuracy ► Book R+ pages 33 to 37

Interval approximation/upper and lower bounds
► Book R+ pages 38 to 43

Density ► Book R2 page 56

Transformations (page 60)

1 (a) (i) A translation of 6 across and 3 down
    You could say a translation of $\begin{bmatrix} 6 \\ -3 \end{bmatrix}$ or of 3 cm across and 1·5 cm down.
   (ii) A rotation
    *Note you are only asked for the **type**.*

 (b) Any three of the quadrilaterals added here.

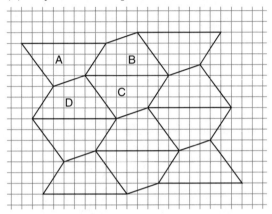

2 The drawing shows one simple pattern you could draw. Other lines could be added, so long as the design fits the conditions.

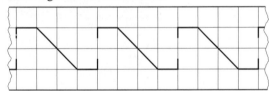

'A period of 4 cm' means that the pattern should repeat every 4 cm.

3 (a) (i) An enlargement
   (ii) A rotation
    *Note again you are only asked for the **type** of transformation.*

 (b) A translation of 5 across, or $\begin{bmatrix} 5 \\ 0 \end{bmatrix}$

 (c) Triangle A and any one of the other three

 (d)

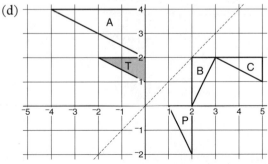

4 (a) $\begin{bmatrix} 0 \\ 6 \end{bmatrix}$

(b)

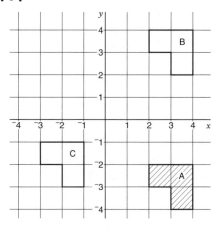

5 (a) Reflection in the mirror line shown
You could give the equation $y = x$.
Note that it cannot be a rotation, because the
corners would have to be lettered differently if this
were so.

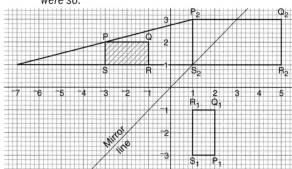

(b) An enlargement, scale factor 2, centre $(^-7, 1)$

More help or practice

Enlargement and reduction ► Book R1 pages 110 to 114,
Book R3 pages 34 to 37, Book R+ pages 46 to 51

Similarity ► Book R1 pages 115 to 116, Book R3 pages 1 to 5

Column vectors ► Book R3 pages 77 to 79

Translation ► Book R3 pages 80 to 81, 96 to 97

Reflection ► Book R3 page 91

Rotation ► Book R3 pages 92 to 95

Loci (page 61)

All answers are drawn half-size.

1

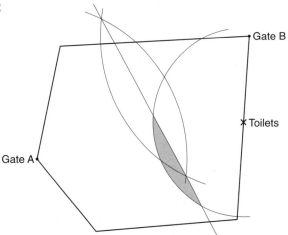

2

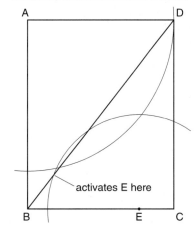

3 The man activates sensor E first.

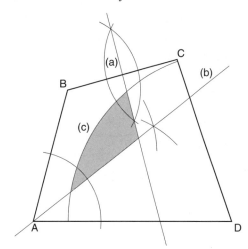

4 (a)

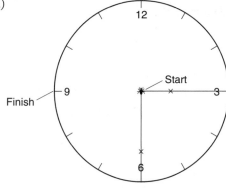

(b)

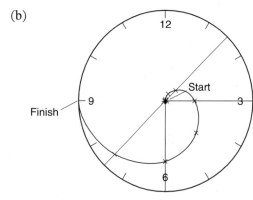

More help or practice
Loci ► Book R1 pages 97 to 104

Scales and bearings (page 62)

1 (a) 1 km is represented by 1 km ÷ 20 000
 = 1000 m ÷ 20 000 *(1 km = 1000 m)*
 = 100 000 cm ÷ 20 000 *(1 m = 100 cm)*
 = 5 cm

 (b) 30 cm on her map
  = 30 cm × 50 000 cm on the ground
  = 1 500 000 cm
  = 15 000 m *Divide by 100.*
  = 15 km *Divide by 1000.*

2 Gradient of 30% = 0·3
 Gradient of 1 in 3
 = 1 ÷ 3 = 0·3333...
 = 0·33 (to 2 d.p.)
 So the gradient of 1 in 3 is steeper.

3 (a) Difference in height = 800 m − 650 m
          = 150 m

 (b) Distance in diagram = 5 cm,
  so on ground = 500 m.

 (c) Gradient = $\dfrac{\text{vertical height}}{\text{horizontal distance}}$
     = 150 ÷ 500 = 0·3

4 (a) Area = 15 × 28·5 cm²
    = 427·5 cm² = 430 cm² (to 2 s.f.)

 (b) (i) Length of 28·5 cm becomes 85·5 cm,
    so scale factor = 85·5 ÷ 28·5 = 3
  (ii) Width of frame = 15 cm × 3 = 45 cm

5 (a) A side of 6 becomes 10, so the scale factor is
  10 ÷ 6 = 1·666...
  Short side becomes
  4 × 1·666... = 6·666... = 6·7 (to 1 d.p.)

 (b) The 6 × 4 and 10 × 8 prints are not the
  same shape (they are not 'similar').

6 Wide side is reduced from 169 mm to 119 mm,
 so the scale factor = 119 ÷ 169 = 0·7041...

 The long side becomes
 238 mm × 0·7041... = 167·5... mm
 = 168 mm (to the nearest mm).

*When measuring or drawing bearings, you will be expected
to get your answers within 1° of the correct angle.*

7

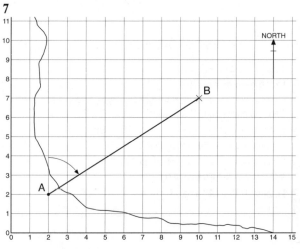

 (a) On diagram

 (b) (i) 9·4 cm (ii) 47 km

 (c) 058°

  *Remember to include a zero or zeros at the front of
  bearings less than 100°.*

8

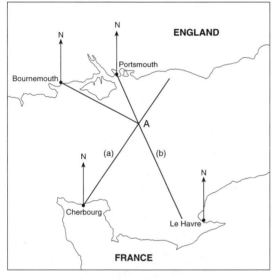

(a) (i) 077° (ii) 310°

(b) On diagram

9

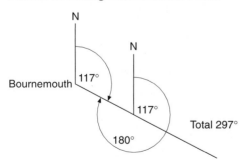

(a) and (b) Marked on diagram

(c) 297°

*The easiest way to answer this is first to draw an **accurate** North line through A, and then measure the bearing. Alternatively you could measure the bearing of A from Bournemouth (117°), and then use a sketch to work out the bearing of Bournemouth from A.*

More help or practice

Scales ► Book B2 pages 1 to 3

Bearings ► Book R1 pages 21 to 24

Angles of elevation ► Book R1 pages 25 to 26

Gradients ► Book R2 pages 46 to 49

Enlargement and reduction ► Book R+ pages 46 to 47

Length, area and volume 2 (page 64)

1 (a) Radius $= \frac{1}{2} \times$ diameter $= 90\,\text{m}$

Area $= \pi r^2 = \pi \times 90^2\,\text{m}^2 = 25\,446{\cdot}9\,\text{m}^2$
$= 25\,400\,\text{m}^2$ (to 3 s.f.)
Make sure you include suitable units.

(b) Volume $=$ area of surface $\times$ depth
$= 25\,446{\cdot}9 \times 12\,\text{m}^3 = 305\,362{\cdot}8\,\text{m}^3$
$= 305\,000\,\text{m}^3$ (to 3 s.f.)

(c) Population uses $12\,000 \times 120$ litres a day
$= 1\,440\,000$ litres $= 1440\,\text{m}^3$.
Supply will last $305\,362{\cdot}8 \div 1440$ days
$= 212{\cdot}0575$ days $= 210$ days (to 2 s.f.)
Don't be too accurate in your answer.

2 (a) πab

(b) If you look at dimensions, the only formulas with dimension of *length*^{2} are πab and $\frac{1}{2}\pi(a^2 + b^2)$. But if either a or b is 0, then the area must also be 0, so πab is the only formula that works.

3 (a) 5 faces

(b) (i) Area $= \frac{1}{2} \times \text{AB} \times \text{BC} = 6\,\text{cm}^2$

(ii) Volume $=$ Area of triangle ABC $\times (12\,\text{cm})$
$= 72\,\text{cm}^3$

(iii) Surface area $= 2$ triangular faces plus 3 rectangular faces
$= (2 \times 6 + 12 \times 5 + 12 \times 3 + 12 \times 4)\,\text{cm}^2$
$= 156\,\text{cm}^2$

4 (a) Radius $= \frac{1}{2} \times$ diameter $= 12\cdot5\,\text{cm}$

Area $= \pi r^2 = 490\cdot873\,84\,\text{cm}^2$
$= 490\,\text{cm}^2$ (to 2 s.f.)

(b) Area of tray $\times$ depth of juice
$=$ volume of juice $= \frac{1}{2}$ litre $= 500\,\text{cm}^3$.

So depth $= 500 \div 490\cdot873\,84\,\text{cm}$
$= 1\cdot018\,591\,6\,\text{cm} = 10\cdot185\,916\,\text{mm}$
$= 10\,\text{mm}$ (to nearest mm)
Be careful to work in cm and only convert to mm at the end.

5 Cross-section of hole is a trapezium of area
$\frac{1}{2}(10 + 7\cdot5) \times 2\cdot5\,\text{m}^2 = 21\cdot875\,\text{m}^2$

Volume $=$ trapezium area $\times 5$
$= 109\cdot375\,\text{m}^3 = 110\,\text{m}^3$ (to 2 s.f.)
More than 2 s.f. is not really appropriate for holes in the ground!

6 (a) $2\cdot5\,\text{cm} - 0\cdot7\,\text{cm} = 1\cdot8\,\text{cm}$

(b) Area of whole circle $= \pi \times 1\cdot8^2\,\text{cm}^2$
$= 10\cdot178\,76\,\text{cm}^2$
So area of moulding
$= 2\cdot5^2 - \frac{1}{4} \times$ area of circle
$= 3\cdot705\,31\,\text{cm}^2 = 3\cdot7\,\text{cm}^2$ (to 2 s.f.)

(c) Volume $=$ cross-sectional area $\times$ length
$= 3\cdot705\,31 \times 300\,\text{cm}^3$
$= 1111\cdot593\,\text{cm}^3$
Weight $=$ volume $\times$ density
$= 1111\cdot593 \times 0\cdot8\,\text{g} = 889\cdot2744\,\text{g}$
$= 890\,\text{g}$ (to 2 s.f.)

More help or practice

Area of a circle ► Book R2 pages 134 to 138,
Book RB+ pages 70 to 79

Volume of a prism ► Book R1 pages 7 to 9,
Book RB+ pages 1 to 3, Book R+ page 2

Surface area of a cylinder ► Book R+ pages 4 to 5

Cylinders, pyramids and cones ► Book R1 pages 6 to 11

Volume of a cylinder ► Book R2 pages 139 to 140

Pythagoras' rule (page 66)

You should always draw a sketch when answering questions of this type.

1

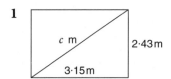

If c is the length of the diagonal in metres
$3\cdot15^2 + 2\cdot43^2 = c^2$
$9\cdot9225 + 5\cdot9049 = c^2$
$c^2 = 15\cdot8275$
$c = \sqrt{15\cdot8275} = 3\cdot9783\ldots$
$= 3\cdot98\,\text{m}$ (to 2 d.p.)

2

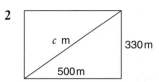

The longest straight line that can fit in the field is along the diagonal.
$500^2 + 330^2 = c^2$
$250\,000 + 108\,900 = c^2$
$358\,900 = c^2$
$c = \sqrt{358\,900} = 599\cdot08\ldots$
$= 600\,\text{m}$ (to 2 s.f.)

A line of 100 pupils is 72 m long, so each pupil takes up $72 \div 100\,\text{m} = 0\cdot72\,\text{m}$.
So 813 pupils will be $813 \times 0\cdot72\,\text{m}$ long
$= 585\cdot36\,\text{m}$. They will just fit in the field.

3

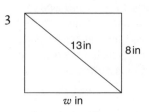

$w^2 + 8^2 = 13^2$
$w^2 + 64 = 169$
$w^2 = 169 - 64 = 105$
$w = \sqrt{105} = 10\cdot246\,95$
Width of screen $= 10\,\text{in}$ (to 2 s.f.)

4

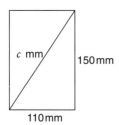

The pencil will fit if it is shorter than the diagonal of the wallet, c mm.
$110^2 + 150^2 = c^2$
$12100 + 22500 = c^2$
$34600 = c^2$
$c = \sqrt{34600} = 186 \cdot 01\ldots$
diagonal $= 186$ mm (to 3 s.f.)

The pencil is 175 mm long, so it will fit.

5 (a) CX is half the radius of the circle, so it is 5 cm.

(b) (i)

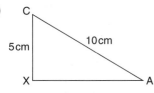

$AX^2 + 5^2 = 10^2$
$AX^2 + 25 = 100$
$AX^2 = 75, AX = \sqrt{75} = 8 \cdot 660\ldots$
$AX = 8 \cdot 7$ cm (to 1 d.p.)

(ii) One of the sides of the triangle is AB.
$AB = 2 \times AX = 2 \times 8 \cdot 660\ldots = 17 \cdot 32\ldots$
Side of triangle $= 17 \cdot 3$ cm (to 1 d.p.)

6

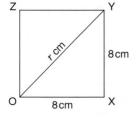

Suppose the radius of the circle (OY) is r cm.
$OX^2 + XY^2 = OY^2$
$8^2 + 8^2 = r^2$
$64 + 64 = r^2$
$128 = r^2, r = \sqrt{128} = 11 \cdot 313\ldots$
Radius of circle $= 11 \cdot 3$ cm (to 1 d.p.)

7

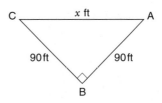

(a) Suppose CA is x feet long.
$90^2 + 90^2 = x^2$
$8100 + 8100 = x^2$
$16200 = x^2, x = \sqrt{16200} = 127 \cdot 27\ldots$
CA $= 127 \cdot 3$ feet (to 1 d.p.)

(b) BD = CA, since ABCD is a square.
So halfway from B to D is
$127 \cdot 27 \div 2$ feet $= 63 \cdot 63$ feet from B.
The pitcher is only 60·5 feet from B, so he or she is not closer to D than B.

More help or practice

Pythagoras' rule ► Book R1 pages 117 to 119, Book R3 pages 106 to 107

Trigonometry (page 68)

1

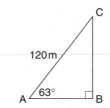

(a) CB $= 120 \times \sin 63°$
$= 106 \cdot 92078$
$= 107$ m (to 3 s.f.)

(b) AB $= 120 \times \cos 63°$
$= 54 \cdot 478859$
$= 54 \cdot 8$ m (to 3 s.f.)
Notice you could have used Pythagoras and your answer to part (a) to work out AB.

In all trigonometric questions it is very important to **use your unrounded answers in the following parts.**
So it is best to write down your unrounded answers before you correct them. However, in this example it is quicker not to use the previous answer.

2 (a)

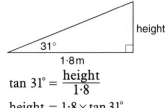

$$\tan 31° = \frac{\text{height}}{1 \cdot 8}$$

$$\begin{aligned}\text{height} &= 1 \cdot 8 \times \tan 31° \\ &= 1 \cdot 0815\ldots \\ &= 1 \cdot 1\,\text{m (to 2 s.f.)}\end{aligned}$$

(b)

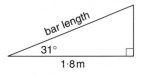

$$\cos 31° = \frac{1 \cdot 8}{\text{bar length}}$$

$$\text{bar length} \times \cos 31° = 1 \cdot 8$$

$$\begin{aligned}\text{bar length} &= \frac{1 \cdot 8}{\cos 31°} \\ &= 2 \cdot 0999\ldots = 2 \cdot 1\,\text{m (to 2 s.f.)}\end{aligned}$$

3

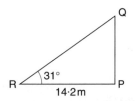

$$\begin{aligned}PQ &= 14 \cdot 2 \times \tan 31° \\ &= 8 \cdot 5\,\text{m (to 2 s.f.)}\end{aligned}$$

4 (a) $\sin a = \dfrac{1 \cdot 27}{2 \cdot 29} = 0 \cdot 55458\ldots$

$a = \text{inv sin } 0 \cdot 55458 = 33 \cdot 68\ldots°$

$a = 34°$ (to 2 s.f.)

(b)

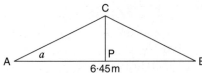

Suppose P is the mid-point of AB. Because ACB is isosceles, the angle at P will be 90°.

Also $AP = AB \div 2 = 6 \cdot 45 \div 2 = 3 \cdot 225$

So $\tan a = \dfrac{CP}{3 \cdot 225}$

$$\begin{aligned}CP &= 3 \cdot 225 \times \tan 33 \cdot 68\ldots° \\ &= 2 \cdot 149\ldots \\ CP &= 2 \cdot 1\,\text{m (to 2 s.f.)}\end{aligned}$$

5

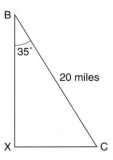

(a) $BX = 20 \times \cos 35° = 16 \cdot 38\ldots$
   $= 16$ miles (to 2 s.f.)

(b) $XC = 20 \times \sin 35° = 11 \cdot 47\ldots$
   $= 11$ miles (to 2 s.f.)

(c)

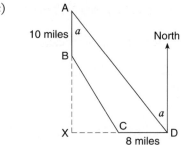

Bearing of A from D $= 360° - a$

In triangle XAD, $\tan a = \dfrac{XD}{AX}$

$XD = XC + 8 = 11 \cdot 47\ldots + 8 = 19 \cdot 47\ldots$

$AX = 10 + BX = 10 + 16 \cdot 38\ldots = 26 \cdot 38\ldots$

$\tan a = \dfrac{19 \cdot 47}{26 \cdot 38} = 0 \cdot 738\ldots$

$a = \text{inv tan } 0 \cdot 738\ldots = 36 \cdot 42\ldots°$
   $= 36°$ (to 2 s.f.)

So the bearing is $360° - 36° = 324°$.

More help or practice

Tangents ► Book R3 pages 6 to 9, 24 to 26
Inverse tangents ► Book R3 pages 27 to 29
Sines and cosines ► Book R3 pages 62 to 69
Inverse sines and cosines ► Book R3 pages 102 to 105

Mixed shape, space and measures
(page 70)

1 (a) Angle EAD = 60°, so angle DAE = 30°

(b) (i) AE = AB   (sides of an equilateral triangle)
AD = AB   (sides of a square)
So AD = AE

(ii) Triangle ADE is isosceles, so
angle AED = angle ADE
$= (180° - 30°) \div 2$
$= 75°$

(c) Angle DEC = 180° - 15° - 15°
$= 150°$

2 (a) By Pythagoras $AD^2 = AB^2 - BD^2$
$= 11^2 - 9^2$
$= 40$
$AD = \sqrt{40}\,cm = 6·325\,cm$
$= 6·3\,cm$ (to 1 d.p.)

(b) Area $= \frac{1}{2} \times base \times perpendicular\ height$
$= \frac{1}{2} \times 16 \times \sqrt{40}\,cm^2$
$= 50·596\,cm^2$
$= 50·6\,cm^2$ (to 1 d.p.)

3 (a) The angle between a radius OP and
the tangent drawn at P is always 90°.

(b) OP = (12 sin 33°) cm
$= 6·54\,cm$ (to 3 s.f.)

4 (a) *Start by sketching the diagrams and joining P and Y.
Mark on any angles you know.*

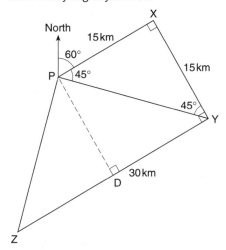

Angle XPY = 45°   *Triangle XPY is isosceles.*
The bearing of Y from P is 60° + 45° = 105°.

(b) *You need to find angle ZPY.*
Drop a perpendicular PD from P to YZ.
ZD = DY = PD
So angle ZPD = 45°   *Triangle ZPD is isosceles.*
and angle DPY = 45°.
So the bearing of Z from P is
60° + 45° + 45° + 45° = 195°

5 (a) 400 m

(b) If r is the radius of the semicircle
$\frac{1}{2} \times 2\pi r = 110\,m$ and $r = 35\,m$ (to 2 s.f.)

(c) Lou's speed = $100 \div 13·3\,m/s$
$= 7·5\,m/s$ (to 2 s.f.)

6 (a) 1 to 10

(b) 100 mm
*The period is the smallest distance at which the
pattern repeats itself.*

7 (a) $\sin 14° = \dfrac{BC}{750}$
So BC $= (750 \sin 14°)\,m$
$= 181\,m$ (to nearest metre)

(b) Time = distance ÷ speed
$= (0·75 \div 60)$ hours
$= (0·75 \div 60) \times 60 \times 60$ seconds
$= 45$ seconds

8 (a) AB = 14 cm

(b) ND = 5 cm (opposite sides of a rectangle)
So AN = 9 cm - 5 cm = 4 cm

(c) By Pythagoras, $NB^2 = AB^2 - AN^2$
$= 14^2 - 4^2$
$= 180$
NB $= \sqrt{180}\,cm$
$= 13·4\,cm$ (to 1 d.p.)

(d) The short side is 2AD = 18 cm
The long side is the sum of the two radii + DC
$= (9 + 5 + 13·4)\,cm = 27·4\,cm$ (to 1 d.p.)

9 (a) Your own drawing of a regular pentagon

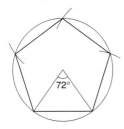

Start by drawing the circle and then measure an angle of $360° \div 5 = 72°$ at the centre. Then mark off five equal distances round the circumference and complete the pentagon. (Its side should be in the range 6·8 cm to 7·3 cm.)

(b) Area of circle $= \pi \times 6^2 \, \text{cm}^2$
$= 113 \, \text{cm}^2 \, (\text{to 3 s.f.})$

Measure to find the height and base of a triangle.

Area of one triangle $\approx (\frac{1}{2} \times 4·9 \times 7) \, \text{cm}^2$

Area of pentagon $\approx (5 \times \frac{1}{2} \times 4·9 \times 7) \, \text{cm}^2$
$= 86 \, \text{cm}^2$

So the area required $\approx 113 \, \text{cm}^2 - 86 \, \text{cm}^2$
$= 27 \, \text{cm}^2$

As measurements are involved, an answer in the range 26–29 cm² would gain full marks.

10 (a) Radius $= 0·09 \, \text{cm}$

(b) Volume $=$ length $\times$ area of cross-section
$= (15\,000 \times \pi \times 0·09^2) \, \text{cm}^3$
$= 381·7035... \, \text{cm}^3$
$= 381·7 \, \text{cm}^3 \, (\text{to 1 d.p.})$

(c) Mass $=$ volume $\times$ density
$= (381·7035... \times 2·69) \, \text{g}$
$= 1026·782... \, \text{g}$
$= 1·027 \, \text{kg} \, (\text{to 3 d.p.})$

11 *Start by adding the information you know to a sketch.*

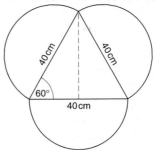

(a) Height $= 40 \times \sin 60° \, \text{cm}$
$= 34·6410... \, \text{cm}$
$= 34·6 \, \text{cm} \, (\text{to 3 s.f.})$

(b) Area $= \frac{1}{2} \times 40 \times$ height
$= 692·820... \, \text{cm}^2$
$= 693 \, \text{cm}^2 \, (\text{to 3 s.f.})$

(c) Area $= (\frac{1}{2}\pi \times 20^2) \, \text{cm}^2$
$= 628·319... \, \text{cm}^2$
$= 628 \, \text{cm}^2 \, (\text{to 3 s.f.})$

(d) Total area $= (3 \times 628·319...) + 692·820... \, \text{cm}^2$
$= 2580 \, \text{cm}^2 \, (\text{to 3 s.f.})$

(e) Total length $= 120 + (3 \times \pi \times 20)$
$= 308 \, \text{cm} \, (\text{to 3 s.f.})$

Notice that the answers to parts (b) and (d) were calculated using 'uncorrected' figures.

12 (a) Distance $= 150 \times \frac{1}{60}$ miles $= 2·5$ miles

(b) BC $=$ AB $\times \sin 20°$
$= 2·5 \times \sin 20°$ miles
$= 0·86$ miles (to 2 d.p.)

(c) AC $= 2·5 \times \cos 20°$ miles
$= 2·35$ miles (to 2 d.p.)

HANDLING DATA

Surveys (page 73)

These are some possible answers to the questions. Your answers may say the same thing but in different words. You may have made some different points that are also valid.

1   (a) The question is too vague. The person being interviewed might not know what sort of answer is wanted or might go on talking for a long time about a lot of different things. If a lot of people were interviewed it would be hard to analyse their responses.

   (b) This is a biased question (a leading question): it tries to persuade you to answer in a certain way.

   (c) This is vague and complicated: people might not know what is meant by 'recently'. It would be better to ask 'Have you bought anything in East Street in the last three weeks?'

   (d) This is suitable. Most people could probably answer it fairly accurately and the results from a large number of people could easily be analysed in a table or a bar graph.

2   (a) The results are likely to be biased towards 'swimming'.

   (b) They would not get the views of students in schools and colleges and people out at work – groups that would make a lot of use of a leisure centre.

   (c) They have tried to get a representative sample, but it is too small, so one or two answers that were not typical could distort the whole picture.

More help or practice

Surveys ► Book R1 pages 65 to 70; Book RB+ pages 61 to 69; Book YR+ pages 12 to 13, 34 to 35, 61 to 62

Sampling ► Book R2 pages 142 to 148

Timetables and calendars (page 74)

1   (a) 0941

   (b) 1 hour 21 minutes
      If you got the answer 161 minutes or 1 hour 61 minutes, it means you used a calculator instead of working out the times as hours and minutes.

   (c) (i) 0849   (ii) 34 minutes

2

3

Month	Letter
January	C
February	A
March	F
April	B
May	D
June	E

It helps to know how many days there are in each month to do this. Start with February, which with 29 days in a leap year has to be A. That means February ends on a Saturday, so March starts on a Sunday, so March has to be F, and so on ...

More help or practice

Time and timetables ► Book B2 pages 24 to 28

Interpreting tables (page 75)

1 (a) The total number of 16-year-olds
        leaving school in 1989 was 640 000.

   (b) The percentage was
        $\frac{50\,000}{570\,000} \times 100 = 8{\cdot}8\%$ (to 1 d.p.).

   (c) (i) The increase was 50 000.
        (ii) The percentage increase was
             $\frac{50\,000}{300\,000} \times 100 = 16{\cdot}7\%$ (to 1 d.p.).

2 (a) The largest loan Mark can afford is £1400
        repaid over 36 months at £49·68 per month.

   (b) (i) The percentage of Marion's total
             repayment is
             $\frac{83{\cdot}28}{983{\cdot}28} \times 100 = 8{\cdot}5\%$ (to 1 d.p.).

        (ii) The percentage is
             $\frac{249{\cdot}84}{1149{\cdot}84} \times 100 = 21{\cdot}7\%$ (to 1 d.p.).

   (c) The total to repay is
        the amount of the loan + the total interest.
        The monthly repayment is the total to repay
        divided into 12 equal parts.
        In Peter's case, the monthly repayment is
        $£\frac{762{\cdot}04}{12} = £63{\cdot}50$.

More help or practice

Tables and percentages ► Book R1 pages 128 to 129

Mode, mean, median and range (page 76)

1 (a) (i) The total time was 112 minutes.
        (ii) The mean number of minutes
             $= 112 \div 16 = 7$

   (b) 38 minutes

2 (a) The mean number of runs is $975 \div 6 = 162{\cdot}5$
        $= 163$ (to the nearest run).

   (b) The range is $215 - 106 = 109$ runs.

   (c) Whitecross has a more variable performance.
        On average the teams score similar numbers
        of runs.

3 (a) The mean temperature in °C is
        $101 \div 12 = 8{\cdot}4$.

   (b) The range for Manchester in °C is $21 - 8 = 13$.
        The range for Vladivostok in °C is
        $25 - ^-9 = 34$.

   (c) Vladivostok has the greater variation.

4 The median weight is 4·7 kg.

5 (a) The median number of minutes late is 4.

   (b) The mean number of minutes late is
        $322 \div 39 = 8{\cdot}3$ (to 1 d.p.).
        Find the total of all the data items first.

6 (a) The mode is 2.

   (b) The mean number of children is
        $66 \div 24 = 2{\cdot}75$.

7 (a) The modal temperature is 4 °C (6 nights).

   (b) The median temperature is 1 °C.

   (c) The mean temperature is
        $(47 \div 31)$ °C $= 1{\cdot}5$ °C (to 1 d.p.).

More help or practice

Mean ► Book R2 pages 9 to 10
Median ► Book R1 pages 27 to 33
Range ► Book R1 pages 32 to 33
Mode, mean, median ► Book RB+ pages 4 to 7,
Book YR+ pages 20 to 25

Frequency distributions 1 (page 78)

1 (a) The mode of these results is 0.

(b)

Number of absences	Tally	Frequency
0–4	ЖЖ ЖЖ IIII	14
5–9	ЖЖ II	7
10–14	ЖЖ	5
15–19	II	2
20–24	III	3
25 and above	I	1

(c) (i) There were 32 students in form 11A.
   (ii) 11 students had 10 or more absences.

2 (a) 5 schools have 6 maths teachers.

(b) 9 have 8 or more.

(c) $\frac{9}{20}$ of the schools have 8 or more.

(d) The number of maths teachers is
$(1 \times 4) + (2 \times 5) + (5 \times 6) + (3 \times 7) + (6 \times 8)$
$+ (1 \times 9) + (2 \times 10) = 142$

(e) The mean number of maths teachers in
a school is $\frac{142}{20} = 7{\cdot}1$.

3 (a)

Height (cm)	Tally	No. of pupils
140–149	II	2
150–159	ЖЖ III	8
160–169	ЖЖ ЖЖ IIII	14
170–179	ЖЖ I	6

(b) 20 pupils were 160 cm or taller.

(c) Number of pupils

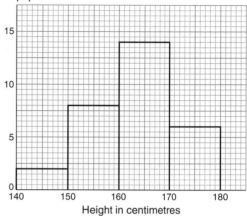

Height in centimetres

4 (a) $30 + 46 + 24 + 10 = 110$ pupils took part.

(b) 30 pupils recorded less than 10 minutes.

(c) 76 pupils recorded less than 20 minutes.

(d) 34 pupils recorded 20 minutes or more.

(e) 10–19 minutes is the modal time interval.

(f)

Time to the nearest minute	Tally	Frequency
0–9	ЖЖ II	7
10–19	ЖЖ I	6
20–29	II	2
30–39	ЖЖ	5

(g) Frequency

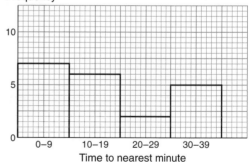

Time to nearest minute

More help or practice

Frequency charts ► Book R1 pages 27 to 29

Pie charts (using a pie chart scale) (page 80)

The pie chart scale is accurate to 1%. You should not give your answers to any question which involves using the pie chart scale to greater accuracy.
You will lose marks if you leave labels off the slices of a pie chart.

1 (a)

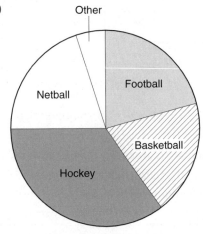

(b) The slice for basketball measures between 16% and 17%. The number of pupils who answered 'Basketball' is 36.
Any whole number answer between 34 and 38 is acceptable (approximately 1% either side of the correct answer).

2 (a) Asia has the largest area at 30% of the total.

(b) The slice for Africa measures between 20% and 21%.

More help or practice
Pie charts ► Book R1 pages 122 to 123

Pie charts (using a protractor) (page 81)

1 Susie sold 180 sandwiches altogether.
Each sandwich is represented by $360° \div 180 = 2°$.
The angle for each type of sandwich is as follows:

Ham	100°
Beef	80°
Cheese	120°
Tuna	60°
Total	360°

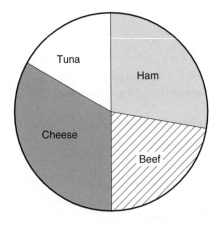

2 (a) The dealer sold 144 cars altogether.
$(56 \div 140) \times 360$

(b) The angle is 165°.

Frequency distributions 2 (page 82)

1 (a)

Length of call (minutes)	Frequency	Mid-interval value	Frequency × mid-interval value
0–5	8	2·5	20
5–10	12	7·5	90
10–15	14	12·5	175
15–20	10	17·5	175
20–25	6	22·5	135
Total	50		595

Mean length in minutes = 595 ÷ 50 = 11·9

(b) Frequency

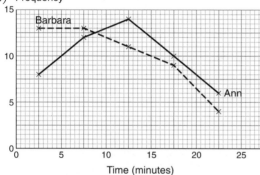

(c) The mean length of Barbara's calls was less than Ann's (10·3 minutes compared with 11·9 minutes).

Barbara spent less time on the phone overall although she made more short calls than Ann.

2 (a)

Length of worm (mm)	Frequency	Mid-interval value	Frequency × mid-interval value
0–40	4	20	80
40–80	25	60	1500
80–120	8	100	800
120–160	2	140	280
160–200	1	180	180
Total	40		2840

Mean length in millimetres = 2840 ÷ 40 = 71

(b) Frequency

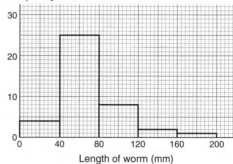

3 (a) *Start by working out the mid-interval values.*

Speed, s (m.p.h.)	Number of cars	Mid-interval value	Frequency × mid-interval value
$40 \leq s < 50$	2	45	90
$50 \leq s < 60$	15	55	825
$60 \leq s < 70$	34	65	2210
$70 \leq s < 80$	37	75	2775
$80 \leq s < 90$	8	85	680
$90 \leq s < 100$	4	95	380
Total	100		6960

The estimated mean (in m.p.h.) is 69·6.

(b) The percentage of cars travelling at less than 70 m.p.h. is 51%.

The probability of the next car travelling at less than 70 m.p.h. is 0·51 or 51%.

4 (a)

Amount collected, c	Frequency	Mid-interval value	Frequency × mid-interval value
$£0 \leq c < £20$	1	£10	£10
$£20 \leq c < £40$	3	£30	£90
$£40 \leq c < £60$	6	£50	£300
$£60 \leq c < £80$	22	£70	£1540
$£80 \leq c < £100$	9	£90	£810
Total	41		£2750

(b) The estimated mean is £2750 ÷ 41 = £67·07.

More help or practice

Grouped data ► Book R1 pages 27 to 28, Book RB+ pages 46 to 52

Mean from grouped data ► Book R2 pages 11 to 13

Cumulative frequency (page 84)

1 (a) (i) 77 cm   (ii) 22 cm

    The first quartile is 66 cm and the third is 88 cm.
    In giving your answer in part (ii), it is always worth
    writing down the values of the first and third
    quartiles. You may earn marks in the examination for
    these even if you get the wrong answer for the
    subtraction – which gives you the value of the range.

(b)

Annual rainfall (r cm)	Cumulative frequency
$r \leq 40$	2
$r \leq 50$	6
$r \leq 60$	11
$r \leq 70$	17
$r \leq 80$	27
$r \leq 90$	39
$r \leq 100$	44
$r \leq 110$	47
$r \leq 120$	50

See graph below.

(c) *Any valid comments on the average and spread will
gain marks. For example:*

The average (as given by the median) rainfall
at both Amber and Baron is the same (77 cm).

The inter-quartile range is larger at Baron
(27 cm).

The rainfall is more variable from year to year
at Baron.

The **range** of rainfall, that is the difference
between the maximum and minimum, is also
greater than that for Amber.

2 (a)

Number of days absent	Cumulative frequency
0–5	32
6–10	99
11–15	**230**
16–20	**273**
21–30	**280**

(b)

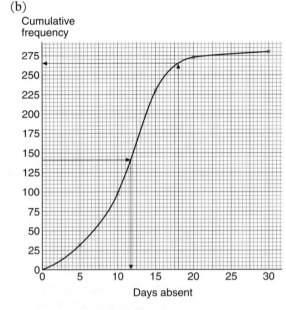

Cumulative frequency

(c) The median number of days absence is 12.
    This is indicated by the arrows which start at 140.

(d) Approximately 15 workers were absent
    for more than 18 days.
    This is indicated by the arrows which start at 18.
    About 265 were absent for less than 18 days.

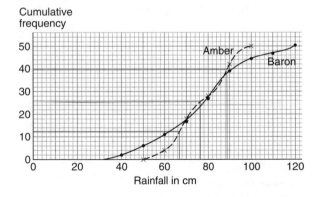

Cumulative frequency

3 (a)

Income (£)	Number of couples	Cumulative frequency
0–50	17	17
51–100	189	206
101–150	215	421
151–200	42	463
201–600	37	500

(b)

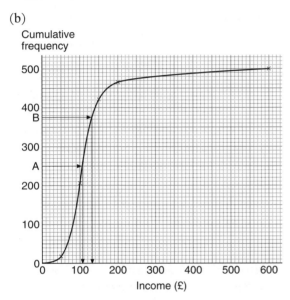

(c) The median income is approximately £110.
This is indicated by the arrows which start at A.

(d) In 1992, 75% of retired couples in Camberton had incomes of about **£135** or less per week.
75% of 500 is 375. The arrows starting at B show how to get the answer from the graph.

More help or practice

Cumulative frequency ► Book Y3 pages 140 to 151
Inter-quartile range ► Book Y3 page 148

Scatter diagrams (page 86)

1 (a) Temperature (°C)

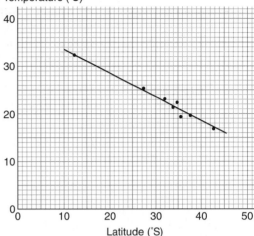

(b) *There is clearly a line of best fit, so there is strong correlation between the latitude and the annual mean maximum temperature. The fact that the line slopes down to the right means that you can make a statement such as*
'The higher the latitude, the lower the annual mean maximum temperature'.

2 (a) Height (m)

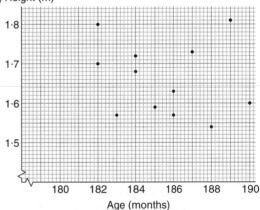

(b) There does not appear to be any relationship between the ages and the heights.
This may be a surprise to you until you remember that these girls' ages are all within eight months of each other. You would expect there to be a lot of variation of heights which had more to do with build than with differences in their ages of a few months.

(c) *Over the age span 11 to 16 years you would expect to see heights generally of older girls being greater than the heights of younger girls. You might reasonably expect to see some positive correlation between age in years and height in metres to the nearest centimetre. An acceptable answer would be 'There is likely to be positive correlation'.*

3 (a) There is strong positive correlation between the cost and the capacity. The bigger the capacity the higher the price.

(b) There appears to be some positive correlation between the length and the cost.

4 (a) (i)

Price (£)

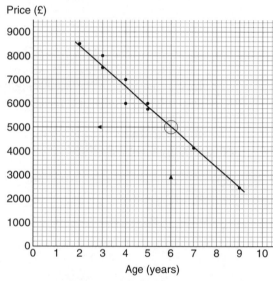

Age (years)

(ii) The older the caravan, the lower the price.

(b) (i) The line of best fit would be in a similar position to the straight line shown.

(ii) The price of a six-year-old caravan would be about £5000.

Depending on exactly where you drew the line of best fit, you will get an answer in the area indicated by the circle on the diagram.

More help or practice

Scatter diagrams ► Book R2 pages 152 to 153

Correlation ► *Kids like us* pages 10 to 11

Probability 1 (page 88)

1 (a) $\frac{1}{6}$

(b) $\frac{4}{6}$ which simplifies to $\frac{2}{3}$.

2 (a) $\frac{1}{10}$ (or 0·1)   (b) $\frac{7}{10}$ (or 0·7)

3 (a) $\frac{3}{8}$ (b) $\frac{7}{8}$

4 (a) $\frac{1}{8}$ (b) $\frac{3}{8}$

5 (a) There are 15 numbers on his card.

(b) There is a $\frac{15}{90}$ $\left(\text{or } \frac{1}{6}\right)$ probability that the first number to be drawn is one of his.

This is the fraction:

$$\frac{\textit{The number of numbers of the kind you want (David's)}}{\textit{The total number of numbers that could be drawn}}$$

If you got an answer like $\frac{1}{15}$, think about why you have chosen the wrong numbers for your fraction.

6 $\frac{1}{8}$

Show the fraction $\frac{50}{400}$ as working. You may get marks for this if you make a mistake simplifying the fraction.

7 0·03

Use the fact that these are the only three possibilities, so their probabilities must add up to 1.

8 (a) (i) 21 times   (ii) 29 times

(b) (i) 0·42   (ii) 0·58

Show the fractions $\frac{21}{50}$ and $\frac{29}{50}$ or the fact that you know there were 50 throws altogether.
Add the two decimals to check that you get exactly 1.

(c) About 42 times   *(0·42 × 100)*

9 It is likely to have been 1200. This gives you the experimental probability of $\frac{612}{1200}$, which is reasonably close to $\frac{1}{2}$, the probability you would expect from a fair coin.

More help or practice

Calculating probabilities ► Book B2 pages 100 to 101, Book R2 pages 124 to 127

Experimental probability ► Book B2 pages 95 to 99, Book R2 pages 124 to 125

All the possible ways (page 90)

It doesn't matter if your lists are in a different order from some of these. The important thing is to be systematic when you make your list, so that you can check it.

1   3   4   5
   3   5   4
   4   3   5
   4   5   3
   5   3   4
   5   4   3

2   Choices

Tee-shirt	Trousers
Red	Blue
Red	Grey
White	Blue
White	Grey
Yellow	Blue
Yellow	Grey

3   S   C   G
   S   C   T
   S   L   G
   S   L   T
   S   F   G
   S   F   T
   P   C   G
   P   C   T
   P   L   G
   P   L   T
   P   F   G
   P   F   T

4 (a)

	4	5	6	7
1	5	6	7	8
2	6	7	8	9
3	7	8	9	10

(b) $\frac{2}{12}$ which simplifies to $\frac{1}{6}$.

(c) $\frac{6}{12} = \frac{1}{2}$

5 (a)   Second dial   (b) $\frac{1}{3}$

	1	3	5	7
2	3	5	7	9
4	5	7	9	11
6	7	9	11	13
8	9	11	13	15

First dial

You could also have done a table that begins something like this.

2	1
2	3
2	5

6 (a) 3582   5382
      3852   5832
      3258   5238
      3528   5328

(b) $\frac{3}{8}$ (if he tries three different numbers from this list).

7 (a)   Black dice

	2	3	4	4	5	6
1	3	4	5	5	6	7
2	4	5	6	6	7	8
3	5	6	7	7	8	9
3	5	6	7	7	8	9
4	6	7	8	8	9	10
5	7	8	9	9	10	11

White dice

(b) No, she's wrong. There are two ways of getting a double 3 out of the 36 equally likely ways, so the probability is $\frac{2}{36}$ (or $\frac{1}{18}$).

(c) 7 is the most likely total.

8

Orange	Lemon	Chocolate
3	0	0
2	1	0
2	0	1
1	2	0
1	1	1
1	0	2
0	3	0
0	2	1
0	1	2
0	0	3

More help or practice
Using tables ► Book R3 pages 10 to 13

Probability 2 (page 92)

It is sensible to check that the probabilities of all the possible outcomes in a diagram add up to 1. In the example with the red and blue balls:

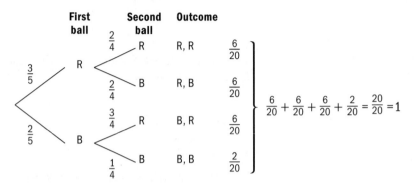

Probabilities may be shown either as fractions (as in the explanation for this section) or as decimals (as in question 4). The rules for multiplying probabilities along the branches of a tree diagram apply in both cases.

1 (a)

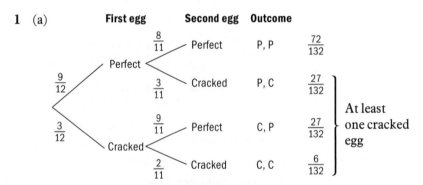

(b) *The probability of at least one cracked egg can be thought of as the probabilities of 'cracked, cracked', 'cracked, perfect' and 'perfect, cracked' added together. This is*

$$\frac{6}{132} + \frac{27}{132} + \frac{27}{132} = \frac{60}{132} = \frac{5}{11}.$$

Alternatively, think of this as the probability of any pair of eggs less the probability of two perfect eggs. This is

$$1 - \frac{72}{132} = \frac{60}{132} = \frac{5}{11}.$$

2

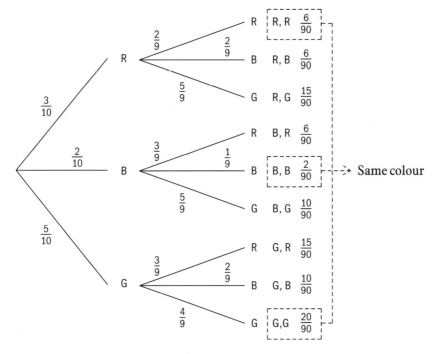

(a) The probability of both blue is $\frac{2}{90}$.

(b) The probability of both the same colour is

$\frac{6}{90} + \frac{2}{90} + \frac{20}{90} = \frac{28}{90} = \frac{14}{45}$.

3 (a)

1st bar	2nd bar	3rd bar

$\frac{1}{6}$ R $\frac{1}{6}$ R $\frac{1}{6}$ R $\frac{1}{216}$ R, R, R

$\frac{5}{6}$ A $\frac{5}{216}$ R, R, A

$\frac{5}{6}$ A $\frac{1}{6}$ R $\frac{5}{216}$ R, A, R

$\frac{5}{6}$ A $\frac{25}{216}$ R, A, A

$\frac{5}{6}$ A $\frac{1}{6}$ R $\frac{1}{6}$ R $\frac{5}{216}$ A, R, R

$\frac{5}{6}$ A $\frac{25}{216}$ A, R, A

$\frac{5}{6}$ A $\frac{1}{6}$ R $\frac{25}{216}$ A, A, R

$\frac{5}{6}$ A $\frac{125}{216}$ A, A, A

2 bars rejected, 1 accepted

(b) (i) The probability of all three being accepted is $\frac{5}{6} \times \frac{5}{6} \times \frac{5}{6} = \frac{125}{216}$.

(ii) The probability of two bars rejected and the other accepted is
$$\frac{5}{216} + \frac{5}{216} + \frac{5}{216} = \frac{15}{216} = \frac{5}{72}.$$

4 (a) The probability that Anwar does not have to stop is
(The probability he goes through the lights)
− (The probability he does have to stop)
= $1 - 0.6 = 0.4$.

(b)

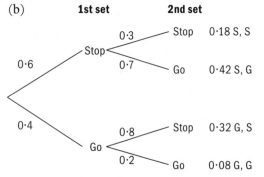

1st set   **2nd set**

(i) The probability that Anwar does not have to stop is 0.08.
(ii) The probability that he has to stop at just one set is $0.42 + 0.32 = 0.74$.

5 *Since it is the coloured balls which result in jobs being allocated, the simplest way to solve this is to work out the probability of picking 2 coloured balls, regardless of their actual colour, that is 2 possible outcomes each time, either coloured or white.*

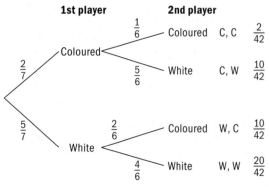

The probability of 2 coloured balls is $\frac{2}{42}$.

The more complicated way is to work out the probabilities of 3 outcomes each time, that is blue, yellow or white.

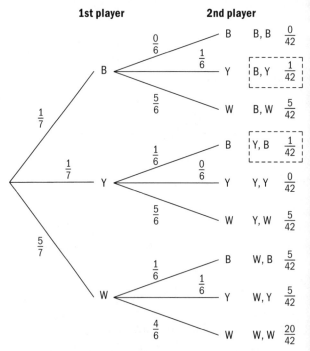

The dotted boxes contain the outcomes that result in a job.

6 (a)

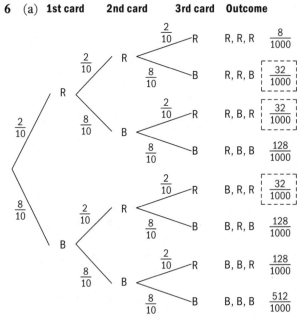

The dotted boxes contain the outcomes of two red cards.

(b) The probability that exactly two of the cards are red is $\frac{32}{1000} + \frac{32}{1000} + \frac{32}{1000} = \frac{96}{1000} = \frac{12}{125}$.

(c)

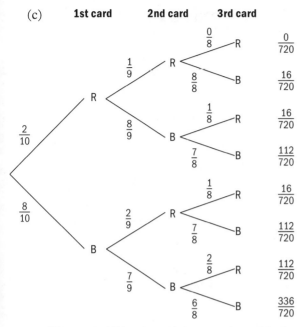

1st card	2nd card	3rd card

The probability that all three cards are black is $\frac{336}{720} = \frac{7}{15}$.

In this question you were asked to draw a whole tree diagram. However, in some questions you may not need to complete the tree diagram to answer the questions. You may even be able to manage without a tree diagram.

More help or practice

Tree diagrams ► Book R3 pages 44 to 47,
Book Y4 pages 78 to 85

Mixed handling data (page 94)

1 (a) In 1975, 10 million (10 000 000 or $1 \cdot 0 \times 10^7$) black and white licences were sold.

   (b) In 1985, 19 million (19 000 000 or $1 \cdot 9 \times 10^7$) TV licences were sold.

   (c) 6·5 million (6 500 000 or $6 \cdot 5 \times 10^6$) more colour licences were sold.

2 (a) There are 28 pupils in the class.

   (b) There are 14 girls.

   (c) 15 pupils have fair hair.

   (d) (i) The probability that the pupil is a girl is $\frac{14}{28} = \frac{1}{2} = 0 \cdot 5$.

   (ii) The probability that the pupil has fair hair is $\frac{15}{28} = 0 \cdot 54$ (to 2 s.f.).

   (iii) The probability that the pupil is a boy with dark hair is $\frac{9}{28} = 0 \cdot 32$ (to 2 s.f.).

3 (a) Rhona's height was 109 cm.

   (b) She grew 10 cm.

   (c) She grew 62 cm.

   (d) (i) She grew most between her first and second birthdays.

   (ii) She grew 14 cm.

4 *Any three of these reasons, or similar ones, would do:*

   The sample is very small compared with the number of voters.

   The sample was not necessarily representative of those eligible to vote.

   Fred only spoke to people on the phone.

   If he phoned people at home on Friday morning he would not have got the opinions of people out at work.

   People do not always vote the way they say they will.

   We do not know how Fred chose the people he phoned. They could be just people that he knew would be likely to vote Conservative.

MIXED AND ORALLY-GIVEN QUESTIONS

Mixed questions 1 (page 96)

1 (a) 118 m   (b) £177

(c) *Split the field into a rectangle and a triangle.*
Area in m^2 = $(40 \times 10) + \frac{1}{2}(16 \times 40)$
$= 720$

(d) $720 \div 14 = 51 \cdot 4$ (to 1 d.p.)

(e) 3 sacks

2 (a) P: 30 fluid ounces, Q: 25 fluid ounces,
R: 1 pint

(b) 160 fluid ounces

(c) (i) Any answer between 0·7 and 0·9 litres
(ii) Any answer between 8 and 9 fluid ounces

3 (a) 12 °C   (b) 8 hours 11 minutes

4 (a) $267 \div 60 \div 60 \div 100 = 0 \cdot 0007416$
Average speed in m/s = $0 \cdot 00074$ (to 2 s.f.)

(b) $7 \cdot 4 \times 10^{-4}$

5 (a) 39·37 inches = 1000 mm
0·375 inches = $1000 \times 0 \cdot 375 \div 39 \cdot 37$ mm
$= 9 \cdot 5$ mm (to nearest 0·5 mm)

6 If the smaller unknown angle is x degrees
$60 + x + 5x = 180$
$6x = 120$
$x = 20$
The other angles are 20° and 100°.

7 (a) If the angle between the ladder and the
ground is a degrees
$\sin a = \frac{9 \cdot 9}{10 \cdot 4} = 0 \cdot 9519\ldots$
$a = 72 \cdot 16°$
So the ladder is within the safety limits.

(b) (i) $8848 \div 9 \cdot 9 = 893 \cdot 737\ldots$
The ladder was climbed 894 times.
(ii) £4470 was raised for charity.

8 (a) Area = $\pi \times 120^2$ cm^2
$= 45\,238 \cdot 93\ldots$ cm^2
$= 45\,000$ cm^2 (to 2 s.f.)

(b) Maximum number of fish
$= (45\,000 \div 1000) \div (15 \div 10) = 30$

Mixed questions 2 (page 98)

1 (a) 19 °C

(b) East

(c) $F = \frac{9 \times 15}{5} + 32 = 27 + 32$
$= 59$

2 (a) $2 \cdot 3 \times 10^7$

(b) $2 \cdot 735 \times 10^7$ kg

(c) $(2 \cdot 735 \times 10^7) \div (2 \cdot 3 \times 10^7) = 1 \cdot 1891\ldots$
Mean mass of paper = $1 \cdot 2$ kg (to 2 s.f.)

(d) The weight is about right for a directory and
is easy to pick up.

3 (a) Area = $\pi \times 16$ cm^2
$= 50 \cdot 2654\ldots$ cm^2
$= 50$ cm^2 (to 2 s.f.)

(b) Area of base = $40 \cdot 96$ cm^2
$= 41$ cm^2 (to 2 s.f.)

(c) $1000 = \dfrac{50 \cdot 2654\ldots + 40 \cdot 96}{2} \times \text{height}$
So height = $2000 \div 91 \cdot 2254\ldots$ cm
$= 21 \cdot 9236\ldots$ cm
$= 22$ cm (to 2 s.f.)

4 (a) $2 \times \pi \times 5 \approx 30$

(b) $0 \cdot 98 \times 0 \cdot 89$ is less than 1, and division by a
number less than 1 increases the answer.

(c) The left-hand side is less than 8×10^8.
($1 \cdot 8^2 \times 1 \cdot 7$ is obviously less than 8.)

5 (a)

Height (h) in cm	Frequency	Cumulative frequency
$15 \leq h \leq 25$	30	30
$25 < h \leq 35$	35	65
$35 < h \leq 45$	48	113
$45 < h \leq 55$	58	171
$55 < h \leq 65$	60	231
$65 < h \leq 75$	19	250

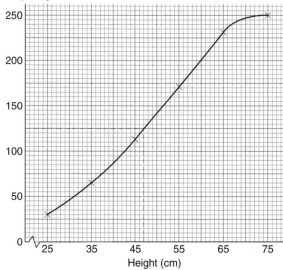

(b) Approximately 140 balls are rejected; that is, 56% of the whole sample.

(c) The median height of bounce is approximately 47 cm.

(d) The answers to (b) and (c) indicate that it was a very poor batch of squash balls.

6 (a) Isosceles

(b) $3x - 30 = 180$

(c) $x = 70°$ and angle B $= 40°$

Mixed questions 3 (page 100)

1 (a) 21 23 25 27 29

(b) (i) 43   (ii) 55

(c)

Row	1	2	3	4	5	6
Total	1	8	27	64	125	216
Mean	1	4	9	16	25	36

(d) (i) n^3 (ii) n^2

2 (a) $3 \cdot 84 \, \text{m}^2$

(b) (i) $1 \cdot 6 \, \text{m}$ (ii) $1 \cdot 8 \, \text{m}$ (iii) $2 \cdot 88 \, \text{m}^2$

3 (a) $3, 6$ and 9 (b) 6 (c) $\frac{1}{8}$

4 (a) $2\frac{1}{2}$ hours

(b) Time = distance $\div$ speed = $x \div s$ or $\frac{x}{s}$.

5 (a) Area in $\text{m}^2 = \pi \times 4^2 = 50 \cdot 2654\ldots$
$= 50$ (to 2 s.f.)

(b) Volume in $\text{m}^3 = 50 \cdot 2654\ldots \times 2$
$= 100 \cdot 5309\ldots$
$= 100$ (to 2 s.f.)

(c) Mass in kg $= 800 \times 100$
$= 80\,000$

(d) $80\,000$ kg $= 80$ tonnes
Number of lorries $= 80 \div 20 = 4$

6 (a) 4 gills $= 568 \, \text{ml}$
$\frac{1}{6}$ gill $= 568 \div 24 \, \text{ml}$
$= 23 \cdot 666\ldots \text{ml}$
$= 24 \, \text{ml}$ (to 2 s.f.)

(b) Percentage increase
$= \frac{1 \cdot 333\ldots}{23 \cdot 666\ldots} \times 100 = 5 \cdot 6$ (to 2 s.f.)

7 (a) $123\,500$ million litres

(b) 1255 hectares $= 1 \cdot 255 \times 10^3 \times 10^4 \text{m}^2$
$= 1 \cdot 255 \times 10^7 \text{m}^2$

The average depth is given by volume $\div$ area. You need to convert the volume of the lake to cubic metres:
$1 \cdot 24 \times 10^{11}$ litres $= 1 \cdot 24 \times 10^8 \, \text{m}^3$
Average depth $= (1 \cdot 24 \times 10^8) \div (1 \cdot 255 \times 10^7) \text{m}$
$= 0 \cdot 9880\ldots \times 10 \, \text{m}$
$= 9 \cdot 9 \, \text{m}$ (to 2 s.f.)

8 The area of the shaded part is $3x^2$.
The area of the unshaded part is
$(4x)^2 - 3x^2 = 13x^2$.

Orally-given questions 1 (page 102)

1 9
   You need to know the square roots of all the square numbers up to 144.

2 40%

3 The line should be between 3 cm and 5 cm.
   You may also be asked to estimate the lengths of lines which are drawn. You should be within about 10% of the true length – don't forget the units!

4 240 m

5 17 or 37 or 47 or 67 or …

6 58

7 27 g

8 $^-2$

9 Between 150 and 200 kilograms
   The best approximation to use is 1 kg ≈ 2 lb.

10 £5

11 4592 pounds

12 Between 4000 and 4500

13 0·68

14 $x = 5$

15 22 m
   Use 3 as the approximate value for π.

16 0·021

17 6 cm^3

18 The angle should measure between 120° and 140°.

Orally-given questions 2 (page 103)

1 326 085

2 54 cm^2

3 £1500

4 $\frac{1}{2}$ or 0·5

5 30 lengths

6 20°

7 70

8 64

9 Between 10 and 15 million

10 6 boxes *You need to round up.*

11 9

12 $^-2·5$ or $^-2\frac{1}{2}$

13 24 taps

14 16 gallons

15 $^-5°C$

16 7·3

17

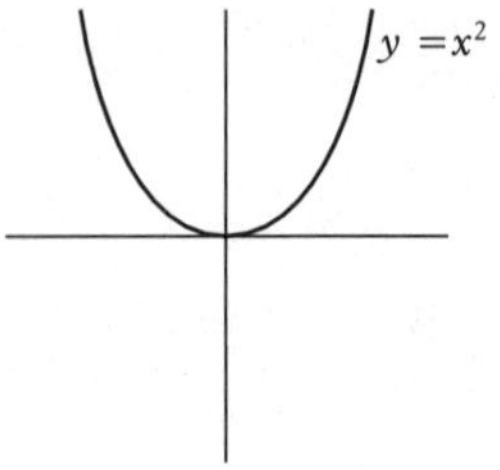

18 3:15 p.m.